THE HOLY LAND

THE
HOLY LAND

AN ARMCHAIR PILGRIMAGE

FR. MITCH PACWA, S.J.

SERVANT
BOOKS

PUBLISHED BY FRANCISCAN MEDIA
Cincinnati, Ohio

To my mother,

Lorraine L. Pacwa

(August 17, 1929–August 22, 1989).

I am forever grateful to Mom,

who was very much loved

by her many friends,

for showing me

the tremendous value of friendship,

in addition for all the care and

generosity of being a mom.

May she rest in peace.

Scripture passages are from the author's own translation.

The illustration credits on page 234 constitute an extension of this copyright page.

Cover and book design by Mark Sullivan

LIBRARY OF CONGRESS CATALOGING-IN-PUBLICATION DATA

Pacwa, Mitch, 1949-

  The Holy Land : an armchair pilgrimage / Mitch Pacwa.

    pages cm

  Includes index.

  Summary: "What's the next best thing to going on a pilgrimage to the Holy Land with Fr. Mitch Pacwa? Being able to travel with him from the comfort of your home as the holy sites come to life through the pages of this book. With stunning images and thoughtful commentary, The Holy Land: An Armchair Pilgrimage is more than your typical travel guide. It also contains: A short commentary on each site, explaining its importance in salvation history A meditation for you to consider, encouraging questions such as, "What can I learn from this place? Why does it matter to me?" Prayers that Fr. Mitch uses on his annual pilgrimages, focusing on a personal faith response to the spiritual events commemorated at each site. Travel with Fr. Mitch to the sites of all twenty mysteries of the rosary, as well as other significant spots in the history of Israel and in the life of Jesus. Whether you've been to the Holy Land, plan to travel there one day, or prefer to stay in your armchair, this classic book will be a beautiful addition to your library"— Provided by publisher.

  ISBN 978-1-61636-613-1 (hardback)

  1. Israel—Description and travel. 2. West Bank—Description and travel. 3. Christian shrines—Israel. 4. Christian shrines—West Bank. 5. Christian pilgrims and pilgrimages—Israel. 6. Christian pilgrims and pilgrimages—West Bank. I. Title.

  DS107.5.P33 2013

  915.694045'4—dc23

                              2013024623

ISBN 978-1-61636-613-1

Published by Servant Books, an imprint of
Franciscan Media
28 W. Liberty St.
Cincinnati, OH 45202
www.FranciscanMedia.org

Printed in the United States of America.
Printed on acid-free paper.
13 14 15 16 17 5 4 3 2 1

SECTION FOUR
East of Jerusalem

SECTION FIVE
Mount Zion

SECTION SIX
North of Jerusalem

SECTION SEVEN
Western Galilee

SECTION EIGHT
The Sea of Galilee

MARE MEDITER RANEVM

PARS TRIBUS

PARS TRIBVS A

ZEbulon ad portum mariu ipse ad portu marium habitabit

Ptolomais

ROGERO VIVION Mercatori probe exercitato, cujus oculis Syria notior, qua nostro calamo, ales firmatas sit, quo, portus fidos, Eolu, Neptunum propitium, omnia deniq; Zebulonis comoda precatur: T.F.

Beth-lehem

VALLIS CARMEL

LEVI
Kattah Kartah

Ajalon
Sepulchrum Elonis

SALTVS CARMELI

CAP MEL

MEL

MON

S

Cain

Dabbasheth

PARS TRIBVS

MERIDIES

Iokneam

LEVI

Naim

LEVI
Rimmon Dimnah

Shimron-meron

Idalah

Maralah

ISHACHAR

Misheal
ASHER

Iephtael torrens sive Shihor Ibnah

Iephta torrens

Iordanus Parus

Zebulon

Canah

VALLIS IEPHTAEL

Tephtael

Naasson

Hanathon

Hukkok

Sephoris Dionesarea

Dothaim

Nazareth

Bethulia

Nahalal Tabor

Sarid

Kishon minor

Chisson Tabor

TABOR MONS

HER MON MONS

Kishon flu.

Bethsaida

Aznoth Tabor

Magdala

Dalman Atha

Iotopata

Ittah-kazin

Gath-Hepher

Naphtah

Tiberias

Taricha

LEVI sive Kedum

Daberah

SCALA MILLIARIVM

Gunereth

Capernaum

ORIENS

MARE Genezareth Galilaeae Tiberiadis

1 2 3 4 5 6 7 8 9 10

Ro: Vaughan sculp:

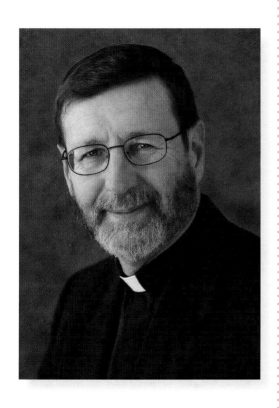

Introduction

When I began my graduate studies in sacred Scripture, I read as much ancient history and archaeology as I could, in addition to learning the languages and exegesis of biblical texts. This desire to understand the ancient land and its sites flowed from my Jesuit background, since St. Ignatius of Loyola urged retreatants to prepare their meditations on the Gospels by doing a composition of place—imagining the sights, sounds, feel, and even the smells of the places where our Lord exercised his saving mission. During my retreats I was aware that these imaginative pictures of the Holy Land came from my own mind, so I tried to supplement them with pictures and descriptions by archaeologists, historians, and other people who had visited the Holy Land. At that early stage of studies, I could only hope to go to the Holy Land one day.

While still a graduate student, I became friends with a wonderful group of people: Sr. Maria Eva Moreno and her friends the Pregovisk family—Stanley, Jacquel, and their son, Nick. They organized lectures for me to deliver in parishes in and around San Diego. In the summer of 1981, Sr. Maria Eva organized a pilgrimage to the Holy Land—Jordan, Israel, and Egypt. Some aspects of the trip were poorly organized, as was a second pilgrimage a year later. A third trip in 1991 was even worse, since the tour company defrauded the group by not providing hotels, meals, a vehicle, or a guide. We made a hasty arrangement of the first three necessities upon arrival in Jerusalem, but it was left up to me to guide the group, and a new phase opened up to me for my many future pilgrimages.

After we complained about the tour company's fraud (later proven in court), the Israeli Ministry of Tourism introduced me to an honest and superb travel agency, Consolidated Tours, run by Christians from Jerusalem, and the chaos never happened again. However, in the subsequent pilgrimages I would frequently supplement the guide's explanation and even take over the presentation at the site. With more study and experience, plus some acquisition of Arabic in addition to my Hebrew, I obtained permission to guide my own groups. As of 2012, I have led fifty-eight trips to Israel, plus ten trips to Jordan, ten to Egypt, two to Lebanon, five to Greece, and five to Turkey. My love of the Holy Land and the many people who live there has deepened, and this book is one attempt to share certain aspects of that love with you.

Beginning with my first trip to the Holy Land, I rejected being a tourist who goes there simply for a few pictures and bragging rights for having been there. Through the last three decades, I have learned to pray more on pilgrimage, leading the pilgrims in prayer and meditation on the biblical events that took place in this land blessed by the prophets, priests, kings, and people of Israel—but especially blessed by our Lord and Savior, Jesus Christ, his Blessed Mother, Mary, St. Joseph, the apostles, and other saints. My primary goal in this book is to share the biblical texts

associated with the key pilgrimage shrines and sites throughout the land, so as to help you deepen your prayer through augmenting "composition of place," that is, an imaginative sense. This book therefore includes pictures of the sites, which are frequently marked by churches and art that further illustrate the biblical events and their significance. I include some meditations based on my explanations of the places that I give when I am on pilgrimage in the Holy Land, as well as prayers modeled on the Collect at Mass, since the idea is to bring the themes of biblical reflection into a petition directed to God personally.

I structured this book geographically rather than chronologically, since that is the way pilgrims make their way around the country. Pilgrims who begin at the top of the Mount of Olives visit the place of the Ascension, the place where Jesus wept over

Jerusalem (Dominus Flevit), and Gethsemane before visiting where Jesus first taught the *Pater Noster*. Traveling back and forth to keep the chronology of the life of Christ would require multiple trips—at least ten—between Galilee and Jerusalem, a practical impossibility on a short pilgrimage. The reader of this book

gets an experience similar to the sequence of visits made by pilgrims who actually go to the Holy Land. One exception is the placing together of the sections concerning the Church of the Dormition (on Mount Zion in the southwest of Jerusalem) and the Tomb of Mary (at the base of the Mount of Olives) because the

texts and prayers are so closely connected. The reader would be lost otherwise, particularly since the text for meditation at both places is the relatively unfamiliar "Passing of the Virgin Mary" attributed to St. Melito of Sardis.

The Dormition and Tomb of Mary are understood in this book by meditating on nonbiblical texts treating Our Lady's Assumption. The only other nonbiblical text I use is presented for St. Ann Church, the traditional birthplace of Our Lady, since only the second-century *Protoevangelium* (or first Gospel) *of James* contains the story of Mary's birth. Otherwise, the texts come from the Bible, primarily the New Testament, though a few Old Testament events are covered. I did the translations from Greek and Hebrew myself, thereby giving some emphases that depend on a more literal translation for teaching purposes. That, and the limitations of my skills, account for strangeness or unfamiliarity you may encounter in the texts.

I hope that you armchair pilgrims—both those who might never have the opportunity to travel to the Holy Land and those who have already been there and want a refresher pilgrimage—may find an opportunity in this book to pray more and come closer to our Savior, Jesus Christ. The Holy Land is a great teacher. In fact, one of my favorite books is *With Jesus through Galilee according to the Fifth Gospel* by Bargil Pixner, O.S.B. His point is that the land teaches us much about the Gospels. In stark contrast with the "Gnostic Gospels" of the second through fourth centuries, which are late frauds that show no contact with the sights, feel, and tastes of the Holy Land, the authentic Gospels breathe the very rhythm of the land. Indeed, pilgrims see the Gospels come alive there and realize that Jesus, Mary, and the apostles did not live in never-never land or some amusement park. Rather, they walked the streets of Jerusalem, of which some portions are now excavated. They passed the same hills, drank from the wells, ate the fish and bread, drank the local wine, and followed the rhythms of seasons, harvests, and religious feasts that pilgrims can still observe in the land. I have been so privileged to have experienced much of this. The land has taught me much, and I keep learning more every time I visit. I pray that you may receive some of the fruit of this learning process through this book.

BETHLEHEM & EIN KAREM

MARE

MEDITER

RANEVM

Ptolomais

PARS

TRIBVS

ASHER

Misheal

Canah

Bethsnemesz

PARS A

TRIBVS

Tepthael

Nauston

Hanathon

Hukkok

Bethsaida

Ganereth

Capernaum

VALLIS IEPHTAEL

Aznoth Tabor

Neah

Remon Chethaaris

Iordanus Parvus

Iepthaei torrens, sive Shihor Libnah

Zebulon

VALLIS

CARMEL

LEVI

Kattah Kartah

Ajalon

Sepulchrum Elonis

Iokneam

LEVI

Nazareth

Sephoris Dionesarea

Dothaim

Gath-Hepher

Magdala

Dalman Atha

Ittah-kazin

SALTVS

CARMELI

Chryphas

Kishon flu:

M ON S

CAR

MEL

Cain

MEL

Shimron-meron

Kishon flu:

Naim

Bethulia

Iotopata

Iaphieh

Hac flu: Dana cium

Tiberias

LEVI

Idalah

LEVI

Nahalal Tabor

Iezer Tiger

TABOR MONS

Kishon minor

Chisloth Tabor

Tarichea

LEVI

sive Keduim

Dabbasheth

Maralah

Sarid

HER MON MONS

ISHACHAR

Kishon flu:

ORIENS

MARE

Cinnereth Genezareth Galilæ & Tiberiadis

SCALA MILLIARIVM

1 2 3 4 5 6 7 8 9 10

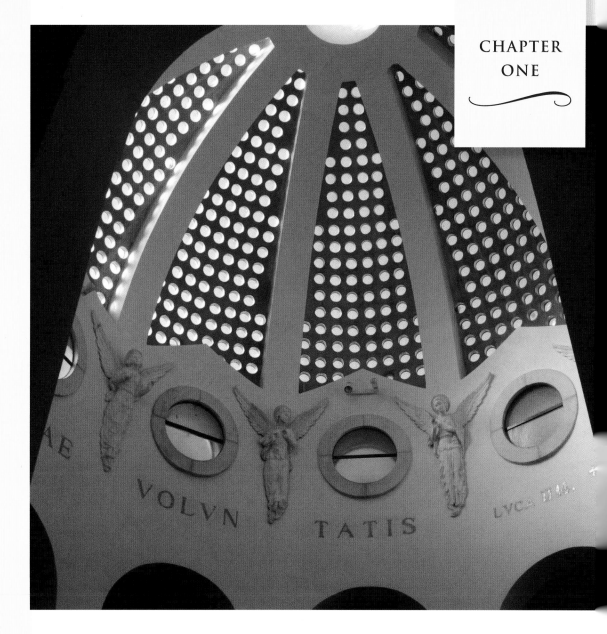

Shepherds' Field

Less than a mile from Bethlehem is the Christian village of Beit Sahur, and there you'll find the Franciscan Church at the Shepherds' Field. As you walk through the gates among fragrant long-needle pine trees, you come upon three kinds of chapels available for the use of pilgrims: outdoor chapels on the ruins of ancient Byzantine monasteries; two caves such as shepherds used to protect their sheep; and the Chapel of the Angels on a small rise above the caves, built by Canadian Catholics and designed by Antonio Barlucci. Over the years I have celebrated Mass at all three, and I cherish the different features each offers.

Outdoor Chapels

The outdoor chapels are formed among the ruins of monasteries from the fourth through sixth centuries. They do not have high walls but are outlines of ancient refectories or chapels with stone-paved floors. Among these ruins is a rock-walled basin identified as a first-century baptistery, indicating the antiquity of Christian worship at this site. Our Christian ancestors spent their years at these monasteries, meditating on the appearance of the angels to the shepherds whom they summoned to go to Bethlehem and worship the newborn King of kings, lying in a manger in a cave that was being used for a stable. The monks chose a simple life on this hill overlooking the fields of Boaz (see the book of Ruth) in imitation of Christ the lowly King, and they worshiped him at Mass, evidenced by the pottery presses for

The outdoor chapel in Shepherds' Field, among the ruins of Byzantine-era monasteries

Eucharistic bread, which Brother Michel, O.F.M., discovered in his years of excavating the site. Today we pilgrims still meditate on Luke 2:8–20 and celebrate holy Mass in this place. Many times over the years I have observed shepherds watching their flocks in the fields below the hill as we read and prayed with the Gospels.

Sometimes a cave chapel is free for Mass and prayer. It is spacious inside, with an altar in front. A stone wall was added to the opening of the mouth of the cave, and the interior limestone walls are black from many years of candle smoke. It can be quite warm on a winter night because the cave holds heat from the people inside. That was, in fact, the reason that shepherds used such caves—to keep warm at night as well as to protect their sheep from predators. A flock of sheep may not deodorize the cave, but they will keep it warm.

Mass is celebrated in the cave chapel

Before the wall was built, when the cave was open to the outside, the shepherd usually slept at the mouth of the entrance to protect the sheep inside. This explains Christ's saying in John 10:7: "Truly, truly, I say to you, I am the door of the sheep." The shepherd would act as a "door," and the sheep would follow his voice and scent to know which cave to enter. For that reason Jesus also said, "I am the good shepherd; I know my own and my own know me, as the Father knows me and I know the Father; and I lay down my life for the sheep" (John 10:14–15). Shepherds typically kept their sheep for years, particularly the ewes, using their milk as a food source and their wool for clothing for themselves and to sell to others. They would therefore have time to get to know each sheep. Having watched local shepherds make whistling and clicking sounds to call their sheep, I could see that they have a caring relationship with them, knowing each one's character. Jesus uses this image of knowing his own to show that his care for us is very personal. He knows our personalities, calling and guiding each of us for our ultimate good and asking us to share ourselves with other people, the way sheep share their wool and milk.

The third chapel is above the caves, an octagonal structure whose location and name—the Chapel of the Angels—recalls the angels who appeared above the shepherds. A large, bronze angel hovers above the chapel door. Inside on the white walls white statues of angels face the altar, beneath which are four bronze shepherds in poses of fear, as if they see the encircling heavenly host inside the chapel.

A favorite element within this chapel is the three frescoes depicting

the story of the Gospel we celebrate here. I like to focus on one character appearing in all three—the shepherds' dog. In the first fresco the angels appear, and the shepherds quake in fear. The dog does his duty and barks ferociously at the angels—perhaps a symbol of those who are unfamiliar with the holy and react negatively to it. The second fresco portrays the shepherds offering simple gifts to the Christ Child, Mary, and Joseph. The dog is sitting, his eyes fixed on Baby Jesus, meditating on him with complete focus, as we all should. In the third fresco, the shepherds are walking down a road, with the cave of Bethlehem in the distance, rejoicing, playing shepherds' pipes, and dancing, while the dog leaps for joy. This dog changed from antagonism, through contemplation, to joy in Christ Jesus. In this way, we can all identify with him.

A large, bronze angel hovers over the door of the Church of the Angels

The Angels Appear to the Shepherds

Pilgrim groups may hear Luke 2:8–20 read at Mass in any of the chapels, or they may commemorate it with a prayer service in which they pray the first part in the cave and the second part in the Chapel of the Angels. If you are praying at home, imagine yourself in the shepherds' cave or in the Chapel of the Angels, and meditate on the following:

There were shepherds in that district living outside and keeping the night watch over their sheep. Then an angel of the Lord stood before them and the glory of the Lord surrounded them, and they were extremely afraid. The angel said to them,

> Fear not! For behold, I announce to good news of great joy which will be for all the people. For today was born for you a Savior, who is Christ the Lord, in the city of David. And this will be a sign for you: You will find a baby wrapped in cloth and lying in a manger.

And suddenly there was a multitude of the armies of heaven with the angel, praising God and saying, "Glory to God in the highest and on earth peace to men of good will!"

In response to meditating on this scene in our hearts and minds, let us consider that the angels' announcing Christ's birth has inspired the Gloria, our hymn of praise at Mass. This reminds us that other liturgical hymns, including the Sanctus, were originally sung by the angels. These songs elevate our thoughts and teach us to join our worship of God to the praise and adoration that are offered him in heaven.

On the other hand, consideration of the lowliness of the shepherds who were called to be the first worshipers of the Christ Child reminds us that God seeks humility in us. Like so many humble messengers, the shepherds did not embellish what they heard but accepted the angel's words with a simple trust that led them to obey what God said. We, too, are called to exhibit a similar willingness to accept God's word and allow him to direct our lives.

Fresco of the angels appearing to the shepherds, announcing the birth of Jesus

Church of the Nativity

The Church of the Nativity is the oldest church in the Holy Land; the Persians destroyed all the other churches when they invaded in A.D. 613. The reason they did not destroy this church was that it contained a mosaic of the Magi, who were wearing Persian-style clothes. The building was constructed at the orders of Emperor Justinian because the previous octagonal church, constructed by St. Helena, had been destroyed by Samaritans during a revolt against the empire. Some of her original mosaic floor can still be seen in the main nave of the church.

CHAPTER TWO

Inside the Church of the Nativity

The main church is entered through a very low doorway; adult visitors must bend down to avoid bumping their heads on the wide stone lintel. Because of the old wooden ceiling beams, rain seeps through the roof and stains the walls. Most visitors are disappointed to discover that many of the mosaics have been washed off the wall by the leaking water. However, the front altar, which belongs to the Greek Orthodox, has a large, beautiful, wooden *anastasis* (screen) upon the bema, separating the altar from the rest of the church. Visitors walk along the right side of the church to the front through a doorway and discover a marble and limestone entrance and stairs, which lead down

A low doorway marks the entrance to the Church of the Nativity

to the cave where Christ was born. Because this portion of the church is shared by the three ancient Christian communities—Greek Orthodox, Armenian Orthodox, and Latin Catholics—public expression of prayer is not permitted as you wait in the long, disorganized line. However, anyone can pray the rosary privately and silently. At this point I recommend that people pray the joyful mysteries to prepare for the visit to the Cave of the Nativity in a focused way, without being distracted by the crowds.

The Cave of the Nativity

Once you walk down the stairs to the cave of the Nativity, the first stop is an altar built over a silver star embedded in the floor that marks the spot of Christ's birth. Pilgrims piously kiss this spot out of devotion to the Savior who was born here. After standing again, you turn to the left and proceed down two steps to another altar, where a stone manger is on the right side. Though unfamiliar to Westerners, stone mangers were commonly used

in stables to feed animals, and many can still be seen at the ruins of the royal stables at Megiddo. Two stone mangers were found within this cave by St. Helena; one was taken to Rome and one remains. At Midnight Mass on Christmas Eve, the Latin Patriarch of Jerusalem places an image of the Christ Child in this manger, where it remains until the Epiphany. If the

A silver star marks the spot where Christ was born

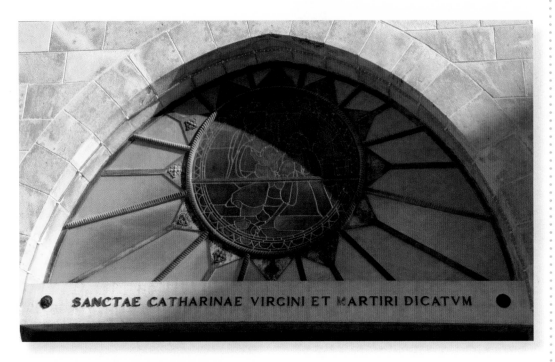

SANCTAE CATHARINAE VIRGINI ET MARTIRI DICATVM

crowds are not overwhelming, you can take a place inside the back of the cave and pray privately for a while, and then go up the exit staircase from the cave and return to the Church of the Nativity. If a priest and group receive permission from the Franciscans, Mass can be offered on this altar.

The Chapel of St. Joseph

Near this exit are the altars where the Armenian Orthodox celebrate the liturgy. As you walk past them, you can go through a large doorway into St. Catherine of Alexandria Church, which belongs to the Franciscans. At the back of this church you will see another staircase down, by which you return to the Cave of the Nativity in the section that belongs to the Latin Catholics and is cared for by the Franciscans. The larger chapel at the bottom of the stairs is known as the Chapel of St. Joseph. Since it was customary for men not to be present when a woman gave birth, Joseph would have waited here until Jesus was born. A passage at the back of this chapel (now separated by a door) leads to the area where Christ was born. Catholics may celebrate Mass in the Chapel of St. Joseph at most hours of the day, and this is a good place to read about the Nativity in Luke and the visit of the Magi in Matthew.

In those days an order went forth from Caesar Augustus to register the whole world. This first census occurred when Cyrenius was governor of Syria. Everyone went out to register, each in his own town. Joseph went up from Galilee, from the city of Nazareth into Judea, to the city of Bethlehem, because he was from the house and family of David. He went to be registered with Mary who was espoused to him, who was pregnant.

While they were there, the days were fulfilled for Her to give birth, and She gave birth to Her first-born Son. She wrapped Him in swaddling clothes and laid Him in a manger, because there was no place for them in the inn.

The birth of Jesus occurred in Bethlehem of Judea in the days of Herod the king. Behold, Magi from the East arrived in Jerusalem saying, "Where is the One who is born the King of the Jews? For we have seen His star in the East and we came to worship Him."

When King Herod heard this he was disturbed, and all of Jerusalem with him. After gathering all the chief priests and scribes of the people, he inquired of them where the Christ was to be born. They said to him, "In Bethlehem! For so it was written, 'And you, Bethlehem of the

land of Judah, by no means are you least among the rulers of Judah, for from you will come forth a ruler who will shepherd My people Israel.'"

Then Herod called the Magi in secret and he said to them, "Go, accurately search out the Child. And when you find Him, announce it to me so that I may also go and worship Him."

Those who heard the king went out, and behold, the star that they saw in the east led them until they stood before the place where the Child was. When they saw the star they rejoiced exceedingly. When they came to the house they saw the Child with Mary His Mother. They fell down and worshiped Him. They opened their treasures and offered Him gifts: gold, frankincense, and myrrh. Warned in a dream not to return to Herod, they went back to their country by another way.

Chapels of the Holy Innocents and St. Jerome

To the left of the entrance to the Chapel of St. Joseph, a small section of the cave contains an altar. This is known as the Chapel of the Holy Innocents. Many people today use this site as a place to pray for the unborn.

To the right of the entrance, another section of the cave branches off into a square room known as the Chapel of St. Jerome. He lived in this room and translated the Bible into Latin there. At the back there is a stairway going up to ground level, an entrance that St. Jerome had cut into the rock so he could go in and out privately. (Today there is a metal grating over the outside entrance.) In the center of the courtyard in front of St. Catherine's there is a pillar with a statue of St. Jerome, who has become an important figure associated with this sacred place.

Ein Karem

Ein Karem, which means, "The Spring of the Vineyard," is considered by tradition since Byzantine times to be the hometown of Zechariah, Elizabeth, and John the Baptist. The name comes from the abundance of springs there that water the many nearby vineyards and orchards.

Also plentiful in this town is the number of convents and churches: the convent of the Sisters of Our Lady of Sion, where their founder, Fr. Theodore Ratisbonne, is buried; the home of the Arab Sisters of the Holy Rosary; the convent of the Franciscan Tertiary Sisters of Egypt; the monastery of the White Fathers; the Russian Monastery of St. Zechariah; and the Greek Church of St. John the Baptist. However, most pilgrims go to the two Franciscan churches here: the Basilica of the Visitation and the Church of St. John the Baptist.

CHAPTER THREE

Statues of Elizabeth and Zechariah welcome visitors to the Church of the Visitation

Outside the Basilica of the Visitation

The pilgrims walk south from the main road, down a street with a few houses and a couple restaurants, until reaching a building named "Mary's Spring." According to local tradition, Our Lady drank from this spring on her way to visit her cousin Elizabeth. At this point, you turn right and walk up the street to a stone driveway with stairs in it. Here it is good to begin praying the joyful mysteries of the rosary, praying just the first decade for now. The climb up the driveway is a bit strenuous, causing one woman on a pilgrimage to say, "You mean she came up here pregnant?" In making the climb, one better understands the passage from Luke: "She went into the hill country...". The view at the top, next to the wrought-iron gate, is worth taking in while you catch your breath.

Above the gate are metal statues of Elizabeth and Zechariah, whose property you have entered. The front wall of the church has a large mosaic of the Blessed Virgin Mary riding a donkey, with Nazareth in the distant background and Ein Karem in the foreground, while angels guard her during her journey. Below that is a courtyard, with a wall covered with clay tiles containing the words of Mary's Magnificat in many languages, including English. You cross the courtyard and enter a small crypt or chapel of the Visitation.

In the Chapel of the Visitation

The theme of the Visitation of the Blessed Virgin Mary to her cousin Elizabeth fills this chapel. Luke reads: "When Elizabeth conceived, she kept herself in seclusion for five months, saying, 'Thus has the Lord acted with concern to remove my reproach among men.'" This chapel commemorates the place of Elizabeth's seclusion among the many summer residences that were customary during ancient times in Ein Karem. The floor mosaic of thatched straw and the ceiling fresco of grapevines evoke such a rustic, summer mood.

There is a tunnel in the crypt with a cave at its farthest end, where there is a short, first-century stone vault and a longer Byzantine vault. It contains the well where, by tradition, Our Lady met Elizabeth.

It is also worth noting the three frescoes by Della Torre above your head in this crypt. The first depicts Zechariah in the temple offering incense at the time of the annunciation of the birth of John the Baptist by the angel Gabriel. The second fresco depicts the Visitation, where a young Mary greets her older kinswoman Elizabeth. You'll notice that Elizabeth is bent over, an artistic way of indicating that baby John is leaping for joy. The third fresco depicts the slaughter of the Holy Innocents, while an angel leads Elizabeth, who is carrying John, to hide behind a rock, an episode from the noncanonical *Protoevangelium of James* (chapters 22—23). The boulder below the fresco is the traditional rock that hid the infant John during the slaughter of the Holy Innocents.

A mosaic on the wall of the Church of the Visitation depicts Mary's journey to visit Elizabeth

Mary arose in those days and went into the hill country with haste, to a city of Judea. She went to Zechariah's house and greeted Elizabeth. When Elizabeth heard the sound of Mary's greeting, the baby leapt in her womb, and Elizabeth was filled with the Holy Spirit. And raising her voice in a great cry, she said:

"Blessed are you among women and blessed is the fruit of your womb! But how is it that the Mother of my Lord should come to me? When the voice of your greeting reached my ears, the baby in my womb leapt for joy! Blessed is she who has believed that the things spoken to her by the Lord would be fulfilled!"

Let us pray.
We pray for all the innocents today being slaughtered by abortion, war, abuse, or neglect. Eternal rest grant unto them, O Lord, and let the perpetual light shine upon them. May their souls and all the souls of the faithful departed rest in peace. Amen.

Because of the angel Gabriel's news that Elizabeth was also with child, Mary took the initiative to travel to the Judean hill country to visit her. Upon arrival, the Holy Spirit took the initiative to fill Elizabeth and John, who was within her womb, with his presence. John leapt within Elizabeth, and Scripture describes this action with Greek term that evokes the joyful skipping or frolicking of sheep. This scene brings to mind 2 Samuel 6:12–23, especially verses 14 and 16, when David danced and leapt before the Ark of the Covenant as he brought it into Jerusalem.

An angel protects John from the slaughter of the innocents

Elizabeth responded with three beatitudes and a question, first declaring Mary and her child blessed, then humbly asking why the Mother of her Lord should come to her, a question that recognizes that Mary's child is the Lord and Messiah, who is superior to her own leaping baby, John. Her last beatitude is directed to Mary, who is blessed because she believed the things the Lord spoke to her. This implies a contrast with Zechariah, who lacked faith in God's word through Gabriel and was made mute as a result—and who still was mute at the time of the Visitation. This last beatitude would later be echoed by Jesus himself: "A woman in the crowd raised her voice and said to him, 'Blessed is the womb that bore you, and the breasts that you sucked!' But he said, 'Blessed rather are those who hear the word of God and keep it!'" The Blessed Virgin Mary heard God's word and kept it and is the model for all believers ever since.

Let us pray.
Lord Jesus Christ, the Father sent you to dwell within the womb of holy Mary by the power of the overshadowing Holy Spirit. She brought you to Elizabeth and your forerunner, John, who by the same Holy Spirit rejoiced in your presence within her. Give us the grace to let Our Lady bring you to us, too, that we may rejoice in you, filled with faith in you and your holy word. May we magnify you from the depths of our souls and throughout each day's actions.

Inside the Basilica of the Visitation

This beautifully decorated church contains many mosaics and frescoes commemorating the Blessed Virgin Mary. The point is to show that "all generations" call her blessed. For that reason, the mosaics on the floor depict plants and animals, who each call her blessed in their own way. On the wall behind the altar are frescoes, one of which shows the woman telling Jesus, "Blessed is the womb that bore you and the breasts that suckled you." Another depicts the various religious orders of men and women who are dedicated to the Blessed Virgin Mary, and opposite that are laypeople bringing models of the great European churches dedicated to her that they have built through the ages. Above that is Mary proclaiming the Magnificat, and the angels are above her.

Along the side wall are five frescoes. The central one shows the wedding feast of Cana, the root of our faith in her intercession. On its left is Our Lady as a mother whose robe encompasses all people of every race, all her children for whom she prays. To the right of the fresco of Cana is one that depicts the Battle of Lepanto, when Mary's intercession saved Europe from a Turkish invasion. The far left panel depicts the Council of Ephesus, which declared her title as Mother of God as a safeguard against the Nestorian heresy, while the far right shows John Duns Scotus defending her Immaculate Conception.

Blessed Among Women

Two prayers would be appropriate here: a litany of the saints who are specially portrayed in the frescoes or mentioned by name for their exceptional reflections on the Blessed Virgin and Our Lady's Magnificat, which is the central theme of the whole chapel.

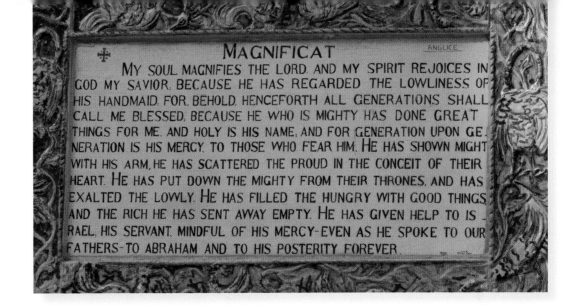

The Magnificat

My soul magnifies the Lord and my spirit rejoices in God my Savior,
because He has regarded the lowliness of His Handmaid.
For behold, henceforth all generations shall call me blessed,
because He who is mighty has done great things for me, and holy is His Name.
And for generation upon generation is His mercy to those who fear Him.
He has shown might with His arm.

He has scattered the proud in the conceit of their heart.
He has put down the mighty from their thrones, and has exalted the lowly.
He has filled the lowly with good things and the rich He has sent away empty.
He has given help to Israel His servant, mindful of His mercy,
even as He spoke to our fathers, to Abraham and to his posterity forever.

Let us pray.
Lord, you filled the Blessed Virgin Mary with the Holy Spirit so that she might speak these words that are now our Scripture and teach us to pray as she did. May we always call her blessed throughout our generation and teach the next generations to do the same. May this prayer always help us see how you help the poor and downtrodden and give us the grace to be your instruments in serving them, too. May we always magnify you in our prayers and actions, for you are the one Lord and God, Father, Son, and Holy Spirit, forever and ever.

The Church of St. John the Baptist

The main altar of the Church of St. John the Baptist attracts our attention because of the statues of the Blessed Virgin Mary, St. Elizabeth, St. Zechariah, and St. John the Baptist. To the left of the church is a grotto, ascribed by tradition as the birthplace of John the Baptist. The five white marble seventeenth-century medallions below and to the side of the altar in the grotto depict the Visitation, the birth of St. John, St. John preaching in the desert, the Baptism of Jesus, and the beheading of St. John. The white marble medallion on the floor under the altar of the grotto marks the traditional spot of St. John's birth.

When Elizabeth's time of bearing was complete, she bore a son. Her neighbors and relatives heard that the Lord had magnified His mercy with her, and they rejoiced with her. On the eighth day, when they came to circumcise the boy, they called him by the name of his father Zechariah. His mother answered, "No, rather, he will be called John."

They said to her, "No one from your family is called by that name." They motioned to his father as to what he would want him to be called. He asked for a writing tablet and wrote, "John is his name."

Everyone was amazed. Then at once his mouth and tongue were opened, and he spoke praising God. There came a great fear on all who lived near them. Throughout the whole hill country of Judea all these matters were discussed. Everyone who heard about it placed it in their hearts, saying, "What, then, will this child be? The hand of God is with him!"

The Church of St. John the Baptist

Zechariah had been told by the angel Gabriel to name his son John. But the angel said to him, "Do not be afraid, Zechariah, for your prayer is heard, and your wife Elizabeth will bear you a son, and you shall call his name John." However, the neighbors and kinfolk thought of the birth of this son in terms of human joy, and they wanted him to be an honor to his elderly father, Zechariah, or some other family member. When they could not convince Elizabeth to give the boy a different name, they turned from her to Zechariah to get his approval of their idea of honoring him.

However, Zechariah was aware of his son's mission from God, and he insisted on the name that Gabriel had given him. Precisely at the moment he insisted on fidelity to God's call and purpose for the child, Zechariah regained his ability to speak. Zechariah's fidelity and the miraculous restoration of speech evoke the correct responses: At this point the visitors fear God and wonder about the boy's mission in their recognition of the Lord's power ("hand") being upon the child John.

Let us pray.
Blessed be the Lord, the God of Israel! He has visited his people and redeemed them. He has raised up for us a mighty savior in the house of David His servant, as he promised by the lips of holy men, those who were His prophets from of old. A Savior who would free us from our foes, from the hands of all who hate us. So His love for our fathers is fulfilled and His holy covenant remembered. He swore to Abraham our father to grant us that free

from fear, and saved from the hands of our foes, we might serve Him in holiness and justice all the days of our life.

As for you, little child, you shall be called a prophet of God the Most High. You shall go ahead of the Lord to prepare His ways before Him, to make known to His people their salvation through forgiveness of their sins, the loving-kindness of the heart of our God who visits us like the dawn from on high.

He will give light to those in darkness, those who dwell in the shadow of death, and guide us into the way of peace.

The Canticle of Zechariah has become part of the Church's Liturgy of the Hours, prayed daily during Morning Prayer. Note that Zechariah blesses God for having redeemed his people by raising up "a mighty Savior in the house of David." The emphasis of this hymn is obviously on Jesus and not on Zechariah's own

son, John. When he does turn his attention to his son, it is to say that he will be a "prophet of God the Most High" who will prepare the way of the Savior. This hymn points out that after his nine-month testing in silence, Zechariah has grown tremendously in his faith. In that silence he has reflected deeply on the Old Testament prophecies, especially after the Virgin Mary's five-month visit to his family. He centers on the coming of the Messiah and the future role of his own son, who fulfills the prophecies in Malachi 3:1.

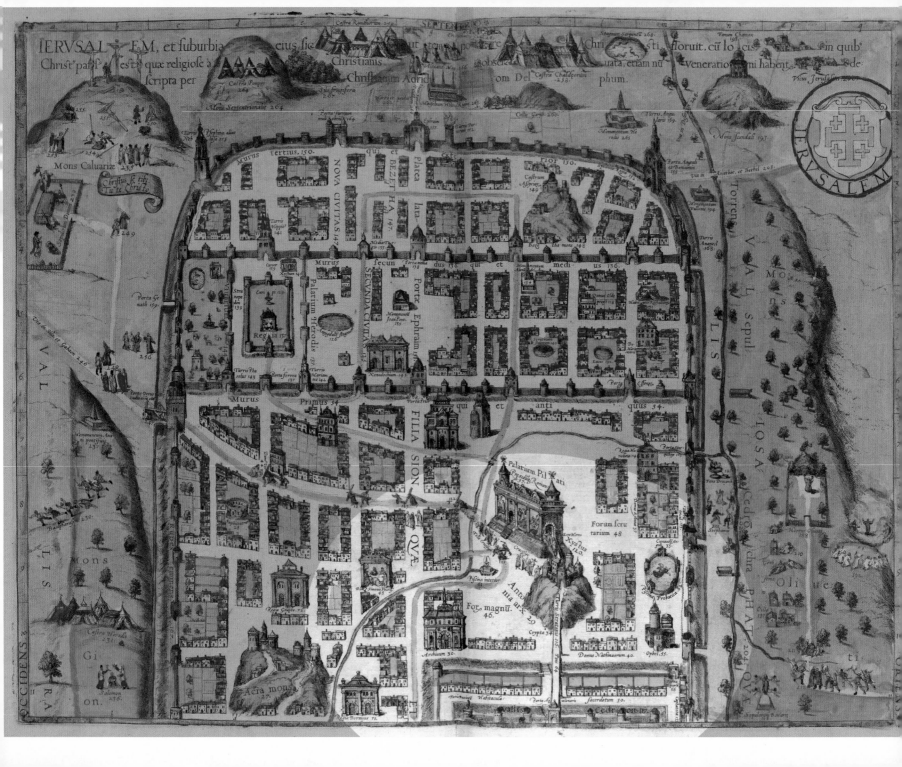

IERVSALEM, et suburbia eius, sic ... ut stan[...] po[...] ... Christi floruit, cū lo[...]is ... in quib'
Christ' pass' est, quæ religiose a[...] Christianis ... obscu[...] ... rata, etiam nũ Veneratio[...]mi habent[...] ... Sede-
scripta per ... Christianũ Adria[...] ... om Del ... phum.

IERVSALEM

Mons Caluariæ 233.

Christus sit tibi, Tu te Christo.

OCCIDENS

VALLIS RA

Mons Gi on. Salomon. 236.

Castra Herodis 231.

SEPTENTRIO

Mons Septentrionalis 264.

Castra Pompeij 264.

Murus tertius, 150.

NOVA CIVITAS 147.

Platea lata

Murus fecun dus 156. qui et medi us 156.

Palatium Herodis 151.

SECVNDA CIVITA

Porta Ephraim

Regalia 137.

Murus Primus 54. qui et anti quus 54.

FILIA SION ET QVA

Palatium Pilati Prætorio Romano

Forum scru tarium 48

Antonia ria arx 29.

For, magnũ 46.

Acra mons 27.

ORIENS

VALLIS Sepul

Mons

TORRENS

Mons OLOSA PHAT QVÆ

Oli uæ re ti

CEDRON

valles Cedr on 117.

St. Ann Church and Bethesda

We enter the Old City through a gate on the eastern wall, which is known as St. Stephen's Gate by Christians, the Lion's Gate by Jews, and the Gate of the Lady Mary by Muslims. A short distance to the right is the property of the White Fathers. Inside their gate is a garden, the Crusader Church of St. Ann, and the excavations of the Pool of Bethesda, where you can see ruins of a Byzantine church and a Crusader church, neither of which has been rebuilt. A number of events from the New Testament and from a Christian apocryphal book called the *Protoevangelium of James* occurred here.

This Crusader Church of St. Ann is preserved because it became an Islamic school after Saladin captured Jerusalem from the Crusaders. It has some of the best acoustics in the Holy Land, so many groups come here to sing. The crypt below the church has part of a grotto where local tradition says the Blessed Virgin Mary was born (the grotto continues east to the Greek Orthodox Church of St. Ann, indicating that both communities recognize the tradition). The New Testament mentions nothing of Mary's birth, but the story is told in a second-century book known as the *Protoevangelium* (or first Gospel) *of James*.

The Birth of Mary

The Protoevangelion of James tells the story of the childlessness of the elderly Joachim and Ann. In chapter 3:2 and following, Ann laments that she has no child:

St. Ann and the child Mary

Woe is me! Who begat me? What womb bore me that I should be reproached and derided by the children of Israel inside the Temple of my God? The beasts of the earth, the seas and the earth itself are more fruitful than I!

An Angel of the Lord stood by her and said, "Anna, Anna, the Lord has heard your prayer. You will conceive and the whole world shall speak of your child."

She answered, "As the Lord my God lives, whether my child is a boy or a girl, I will dedicate it to the Lord my God to minister all life long to Him in holy things."

An angel of the Lord also appeared to Joachim and said, "The Lord God has heard your prayer. Hurry to your home, for your wife Anna will conceive."

Joachim stayed at home on the first day after his arrival there. The next day he offered sacrifices to the Lord in the Temple. Nine months later St. Ann gave birth and asked the midwife: "What have I brought forth?" The midwife answered, "A girl!" Then St. Ann said, "This day the Lord has magnified my soul!" When the days of her purification were completed, she suckled the child and called her, "Mary."

When the child was a year old, St. Joachim made a great feast for the priests, scribes, elders and people. St. Joachim offered the girl to the chief priests, who blessed her, saying, "May the God of our fathers bless this girl and give her a name that is famous and lasting through all generations."

And all the people replied, "Amen!"

An icon of Mary's birth decorates the Grotto of Mary's Nativity

Obviously, this later text attributed to St. James has the New Testament and the spread of the Church in mind in a number of ways. This episode begins with St. Ann lamenting her childlessness, a state much regretted in the ancient world in general, but especially in Israel, where the first commandment (of the 613 laws in the Torah) that God spoke to the first humans was "Be fruitful and multiply."

Though it was through no fault of her own, St. Ann could not fulfill that command.

This state changed when God sent his angel to announce that the Lord had heard her prayer and would answer it. As occurs often in the Bible, God waits until old age to answer the prayer for a child in order to make it clear that the child is God's gift and not merely a human effort. This is especially true of this most special child of whom "the whole world shall speak." An angel told Joachim to go home to his wife, since the conception of this child would take place in the usual way, and nine months later the birth occurred. When Mary was born, St. Ann said that her soul magnified the Lord, clearly a reference to the Blessed Virgin's own Magnificat at her visitation to the elderly Elizabeth, who was pregnant at that moment. Magnifying the Lord is the proper response to God's activity in our lives, particularly when it seems so far beyond the accomplishments of mere human nature.

Pool of Bethesda

Outside the Church of St. Ann are the excavations of the Pool of Bethesda. At the east end are the ruins of a Byzantine church, and the structure in the center of the pool is

a Crusader church. Various pagan shrines can be found among the ruins. At the west end of the pool is a stone wall, still partially covered by plaster. This may be the eighth-century wall of the upper pool mentioned in Isaiah, the location of one of the most famous prophecies of the Messiah and his mother in the Old Testament.

When Ahaz, the son of Jotham, the son of Uzziah, was the king of Judah, Rezin the king of Aram (Syria) and Pekah son of Remaliah the king of Israel, went up to Jerusalem to make war against her. However, they were unable to fight the war. The house of David was told, "Aram has rested with Ephraim [Northern Israel]." His heart shuddered and the heart of his people fluttered like the trees of the forest before the wind.

Then the LORD said to Isaiah,

Go meet Ahaz, you and your son Remnant-Will-Return [Shear-Jashub], at the end of the conduit of the Upper Pool, at the highway of the Fullers' Field. Say to him, "Be on guard and keep quiet; fear not and do not let your heart be weak on account of these two stumps of fire brands. Their plan will not stand and will not happen.'"

Then the LORD spoke again to Ahaz: "Ask for a sign from the LORD your God for yourself. Let the request be deep or high above."

But Ahaz said, "I will not ask and I will not test the LORD."

Then Isaiah said,

Listen, House of David: Is it too small for you to weary men that you also weary my God? Therefore the Lord Himself will give you a sign: Behold, a virgin shall conceive and bear a son, and she will call his name "Emmanuel." Curds and honey will he eat when he knows how to refuse evil and choose good. For before the lad knows how to refuse evil and choose good, the land will forsake its two kings, whom you dread.

Politics in the eighth century B.C. is the background of this prophecy. An Assyrian general had usurped power from his king in 745 B.C. and began an aggressive push to conquest western Asia. Rezin of Aram and Pekah of Israel formed an alliance against Assyria and asked King Ahaz of Judah to join, but he refused. Rezin and Pekah decided to overthrow Ahaz in 734 B.C. At this point the Lord sent Isaiah and his son to instruct Ahaz to remain quiet and be without fear because Rezin and Pekah would fail. When Ahaz refused to ask for a sign, Isaiah offered the sign that the virgin will conceive and bear a son, Emmanuel, meaning "God is with us." The full significance of the sign would not be understood until the Virgin Mary conceived Jesus, the Son of God.

Let us pray.
Lord, the war with Rezin and Pekah devastated the land's produce, leaving only wild honey and curds to eat. So also, sin has devastated the whole earth since the fall of Adam and Eve. You, Lord Jesus, took flesh in the womb of the Virgin Mary to save us from that devastation of evil and sin. Teach us to have faith in you and stand firmly against sin so that, like the sinless Virgin Mary, we might be reborn into the eternal joys of heaven. Amen.

Jesus Heals the Paralyzed Man on a Sabbath

There was a feast of the Jews, so Jesus went up to Jerusalem. There is a pool in Jerusalem near the Sheep Gate called Bethesda in Hebrew, which has five porticoes. In them was set a large crowd of the sick, blind, lame, and paralyzed, waiting for the movement of the water. For an angel came down in the pool at the right time and stirred the water. Then the first one entering after the stirring of the water became healthy, from whatever sickness he was constrained.

A certain man was there who was sick for thirty-eight years. When Jesus saw this man, knowing that he had already been there for a long time, He said to him, "Do you want to be healthy?"

The sick man answered Him, "Lord, I do not have a man, so that when the water is stirred up, he may put me into the pool. While I am coming, another comes down before me."

Jesus said to him, "Get up, pick up your mat and walk." Immediately the man became healthy, took up his mat and walked.

John mentions that the Pool of Bethesda had five porticoes. The excavations on the property of St. Ann's explain this statement, since there are four sides of the square pool, plus a central portico that ran east to west down the middle of the pool.

The paralytic had been waiting for a healing since before Christ was born, but he was alone, and no one helped him into the water. Jesus approached him with an offer of health, but the paralytic could only describe the problem of not having any help. Jesus responded with a command to walk and pick up his mat, and the healing occurred simply by that word.

Let us pray.
Lord Jesus Christ, true Son of the Father, you have the authority to free us from sin and from sickness. By your stripes we are healed: your suffering and passion bring us both freedom from sin and healing of diseases, as Isaiah foretold about you. Heal us this day so that we may be strong enough to serve you and proclaim your Good News to the whole world. May our healing be for your greater glory and praise, now and forever. Let us pray for healing by praying as Jesus taught us. Amen.

The Chapels of Flagellation & Condemnation

After leaving St. Ann's and the Pool of Bethesda, pilgrims walk west along a stone-paved street to the property of the Franciscans, a couple blocks down and on the right side of the street. This property contains a school, a museum (usually closed), and two chapels, one on either side of a courtyard.

The chapel on the right side of the courtyard is dedicated to Jesus's scourging and crowning with thorns. The altar rests on a pillar in honor of the scourging, and the ceiling is a mosaic of a crown of thorns. The beautiful windows are made from alabaster, not glass, and depict Christ's scourging and crowning, the release of Barabbas, and Pilate washing his hands.

Pilate then had Jesus scourged. The soldiers wove a crown of thorns and placed it on His head and they clothed Him with a purple cloak. They said to Him, "Hail, King of the Jews!"

Then they struck Him. Again Pilate went out and said to the crowd, "See, I will bring Him outside to you, that you may know that I have found no charge against Him." Therefore he brought Jesus out, wearing the crown of thorns and the purple garment, and he said to them, "Behold the man!"

However, when the chief priests and elders saw Him, they cried out, "Crucify Him, crucify Him!"

First, we note that the scourging of Jesus occurs in the context of a trial before Pilate. As the dispute between Pilate and the Jewish leaders makes clear, the antagonism of Jesus's accusers becomes ever stronger, despite the lack of evidence of a crime

Alabaster window of Jesus being scourged

against Roman law. Pilate hopes to assuage the anger by scourging Jesus. The soldiers go a step beyond the mandatory scourging and add a crown of thorns and purple cloak, mocking Jesus's kingship on their own initiative. Pilate and the soldiers probably knew nothing of the prophet Isaiah, but here, as elsewhere, they contribute to the fulfillment of his prophecies. "He was wounded for our rebellion, struck for our iniquity, upon him was the chastisement that makes us whole, and by his stripes we are healed." Also, "I gave my back to the smiters, and my cheeks to those who make them bare; my face I did not hide from shame and spitting."

These prophecies indicate that Christ's sufferings are oriented to healing those who have faith in him and to the forgiveness of sins. This orientation helps explain the importance of Christ's wounds still being visible to the apostles on the first Easter and beyond: the wounds in his hands, feet, and side are glorified and bring healing for all eternity. Our reflection on the scourging helps us seek healing for the various sins of the flesh; the crowning with thorns helps us seek forgiveness for our sins of pride by virtue of Jesus's humiliation by the soldiers.

Second, Pilate makes his famous declaration, "Behold the man! *Ecce homo!*" He intends this to placate the crowd, but it only infuriates them to demand crucifixion. They charge Jesus with making himself God, an accusation that goes back to Bethesda when he called God his Father and to the previous Feast of Tabernacles when he said, "Before Abraham came to be, I Am." This accusation makes Pilate even more afraid, and he wants to let Jesus go. But he cannot. Ultimately the crowd's anger overcomes his better judgment, and he lets Jesus be crucified.

Let us pray.
Lord Jesus, you took on the intense suffering of the scourging, plus the physical pain of the thorns and the humiliation by the soldiers. I cannot comprehend the depth of hurt you experienced, a suffering I would not inflict on an animal, let alone you. Yet you endured this in a noble silence so that my sins might be forgiven. May the tearing of your flesh bring me healing for the effects of the sins I have committed. Grant me a holy grief for all you have endured for me so that my understanding of your gift might keep me from sinning again. Holy Lord Jesus, have mercy on me, a sinner. Amen.

The Chapel of the Condemnation

The second chapel on the property is across the courtyard from the chapel dedicated to the flagellation and crowning with thorns. A careful look at the floor of the Chapel of the Condemnation shows a number of ancient, large pavement stones, which are part of a pavement that continues west to the Ecce Homo Convent across the street. This stone pavement was part of the interior pavement of the Fortress Antonia, which was built by Herod the Great and named after his friend Marc Antony. Although the stone pavement there today is actually from the 130s, a hundred years after Christ's condemnation, when a new underground cistern was dug inside the fort, it points to the certain existence of the fort at the time of Christ. The fort's existence explains why the condemnation, scourging, and the beginning of the Way of the Cross are located here according to tradition since Byzantine times. Furthermore, the presence here of old prison cells explains the ready availability of Barabbas and the two thieves for judgment and execution with Jesus.

The Jewish leaders cried out, "If you release this man, you are no friend of Caesar's. Everyone who makes himself king sets himself against Caesar."

When Pilate heard these words, he led Jesus outside and he sat on the platform at the place called Lithostratos (stone pavement), in Hebrew Gabbatha. It was the Day of Preparation for the Passover, about midday. He said to them, "Behold your King!"

At that point they cried out, "Away with Him, away with Him, crucify Him!"

Pilate said to them, "Shall I crucify your King?"

The high priests answered, "We have no king but Caesar."

Then Pilate saw that nothing availed but rather that a riot was beginning to form. He took water and washed his hands in the presence of the crowd, saying, "I am innocent of this man's blood." Then he handed Him over to them to be crucified.

Let us pray.
Lord, righteous Judge of the living and the dead, in order to prevent the condemnation of the world you allowed the world to condemn you. By your condemnation free us from the sentence our sins deserve. Give us the grace to be patient with those who judge us, and free us from proudly judging the people around us. Amen.

Above the altar in the Chapel of the Condemnation is a bas-relief of Pilate washing his hands and of Jesus being given the cross. On the wall opposite the door is another scene of the Blessed Mother watching Jesus take up the cross, while St. Mary Magdalene tries to comfort her and St. John lifts his cloak to shield her from seeing Jesus begin the Way of the Cross.

Let us pray.
Lord, it is horrible to consider that here you began to carry the wood on which you would be killed. The reality of the death you had contemplated in Gethsemane now takes fearful reality. Yet, we remember your words: "I lay down My life to take it up again; no one takes it from Me, I lay it down on My own" (John 10:17–18). We thank you for this great gift, which sets us free from sin and self-centeredness. We now offer to follow you by taking up our own crosses, too. Amen.

The Via Dolorosa

When we leave the Chapel of the Condemnation, a left turn on the street takes us along the Via Dolorosa, as the various street signs indicate. We will focus here on the chapels that are found along the way where you can pray some of the stations of the Way of the Cross.

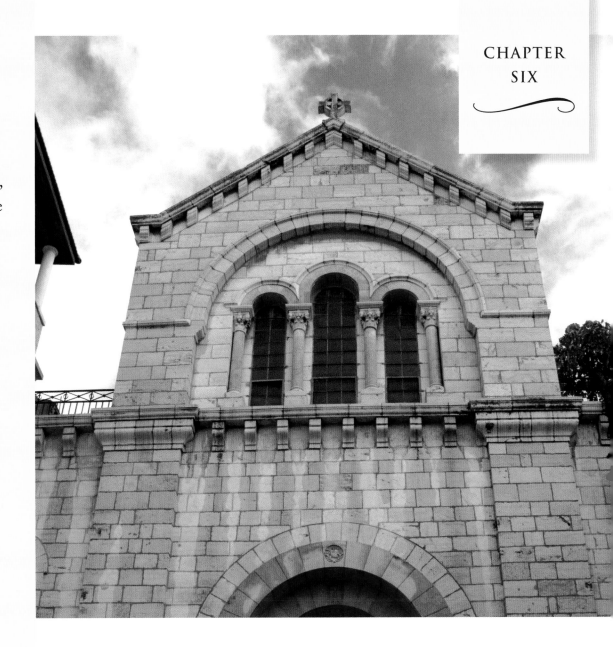

Let us pray.

Lord Jesus Christ, by your weakness we are made strong; by your fall, a fallen human race is lifted up from its sin. The cross crushed you so that our guilt might be removed and that we might be made whole. Heal us of our weaknesses and keep us from straying from you, who are Lord forever and ever. Amen.

The Third Station: Jesus Falls the First Time

After walking a couple blocks, we come to a T intersection at El Wad Street, where the Via Dolorosa takes a sharp turn south. Immediately you will see the Chapel of the Third Station, which was built by Polish soldiers who had walked to the Holy Land from their homeland after it was invaded by the Germans on the west and the Russians on the east during World War II. As we enter this chapel, we see a statue of Jesus falling under the weight of the cross at the front, while a nearby mural of Polish people, who had experienced the fall of their nation to the forces of Nazism and Communism, portrays their prayer and faith in Jesus. Just as those soldiers saw their suffering in the light of Jesus falling down, so might we consider our own difficulties.

He was despised and rejected by men
A man of grief, knowing infirmity.
Like one from whom they hide their
    faces.
He was despised, and we did not
    consider Him.
Yet He bore our infirmities,
He carried our diseases.
But we considered Him stricken,
Struck by God and afflicted.
Yet He was pierced for our rebellion,
Crushed for our guilt.
The chastisement that makes us whole
    was upon Him
And by His stripes we were healed.
All of us had gone astray like sheep,
Each of us turned to his own way.
But the Lord placed upon Him the guilt
    of us all.

The Fourth Station: Jesus Meets Mary, His Blessed Mother

Today we can walk through the Chapel of the Third Station into the lower part of the Armenian Rite Catholic Church, whose members care for that chapel and the Chapel of the Fourth Station, when Jesus meets his Blessed Mother. In the lower church is a Eucharistic Adoration chapel, open to anyone who wants to spend time before the Blessed Sacrament exposed in a large, beautiful monstrance. Just outside that chapel is a life-size statue of Jesus meeting his Mother. In front of the statue is a fourth-century mosaic floor with two mosaic sandals depicted to mark the spot where it is believed Mary stood. Up a nearby stairway you enter the main church of the Armenian Catholic parish, where a painting of Jesus's first fall is on one wall and Jesus meeting his Mother is on the other. After leaving the church, you'll turn south again on El Wad Street to continue the Via Dolorosa, and you'll notice a stone bas-relief of Jesus meeting his Blessed Mother. All of these remind us of the words Simeon speaks to Mary.

Behold, He is set for the fall and the rise of many in Israel and as a sign of contradiction. A sword will pierce your soul so that the thoughts of many hearts might be revealed.

Let us pray.
Truly, O blessed Mother, a sword has pierced your heart. For only by passing through your heart could the sword enter the flesh of your Son. Indeed, after your Son, Jesus—who belongs to everyone but is especially yours—gave up his life, the cruel spear tore open his side. Thus the violence of sorrow has cut through your

heart, and we rightly call you more than martyr, since the effect of compassion in you has gone beyond the endurance of physical suffering. Amen.

(See St. Bernard of Clairvaux's Sermon on the Assumption from the Office of Readings for the Feast of Our Lady of Sorrows.)

The Fifth Station: Simon of Cyrene Is Made to Carry the Cross

A short distance from the Fourth Station is another T intersection, where the Via Dolorosa turns west and starts to ascend. At that corner stands a small Franciscan chapel built in 1895, next to the oldest Franciscan house in Jerusalem dating from A.D. 1229. A Latin inscription on the lintel of the chapel door identifies the place as the Fifth Station.

Simon was a foreigner from the North African town of Cyrene. The first-century Jewish historian Josephus wrote that many Jews lived there, and Simon's Jewish name indicates he was among them. Perhaps he was a pilgrim for the Passover, or perhaps he lived in Jerusalem. We read in the Gospels what kept him from the oblivion of history: "They forced a certain passerby who was coming from the field, Simon the Cyrenean, the father of Alexander and Rufus, to carry His cross." And, "They placed the cross on him to carry it behind Jesus."

Perhaps the reason St. Mark mentioned Simon's sons is that he may have known them in Rome, where he wrote his Gospel. Evidence for this may be found in Romans, where St. Paul wrote, "Greet Rufus, eminent in the Lord, also his mother and mine," apparently well-known members of the Church there.

Let us pray.
Lord Jesus Christ, give us compassion for you, who are present in our neighbors. Make our service to others be offered with as much love and concern as if we were Simon lifting your cross. And may all our service be for your greater glory and praise. Amen.

The Sixth Station: Veronica Wipes Jesus's Face

As we continue on the Via Dolorosa, the street begins to ascend the hill on which the western part of the Old City rests. Along this street is the Greek Catholic Chapel of St. Veronica, which is now maintained by the Little Sisters of Jesus. An ancient pillar that is now built into the exterior chapel wall marks the station, but the sisters permit pilgrims to enter their little chapel as well, where an icon of the Face of Jesus on Veronica's veil sits below the front altar.

Here we can remember that Christ submitted to his torment for our sake, suffering in fulfillment of the Scriptures, as we read from the prophet Isaiah:

The Lord GOD has given me a tongue of
  the well trained
to know how to address to the weary a
  word which will rouse them.
Morning by morning He awakens My ear
  to listen like the well trained.
The Lord GOD has opened My ear and I
  have not rebelled,
I have not turned back.
I gave My back to those who strike Me
and My cheeks to those who pluck My
  beard.

I did not hide My face from humiliation or
  spitting.
The Lord GOD will help Me
Therefore I will not be humiliated.
Therefore I have set My face like flint,
And I know that I will not be put to
  shame.

For I have born reproach because of You,
Humiliation covers My face.
Zeal for Your house has consumed Me;
The reproaches of those who reproach
  You have fallen on Me.

Let us pray.
As Christ our Lord passes by, a woman compassionately wipes his bruised and bloodied face. He rewards her by leaving the image of his face on her veil, so she is called Veronica—meaning "true image." May we show Christ compassion by seeing his face in all who suffer and by doing what we can to alleviate their suffering. Amen.

The Seventh Station: Jesus Falls the Second Time

The Chapel of the Seventh Station is located where the Via Dolorosa meets Suq Khan ez-Zeit Street, the location of a famous marketplace. The Roman numerals VII stand over the door of this chapel, also called the Chapel of the Judgment Gate, which was built by the Franciscans in 1875. According to Christian tradition, the decree of condemnation was posted on the gate that was in this spot as Jesus passed through, and here Jesus fell again.

Pilgrims carry the cross along the Via Dolorosa, which winds through the narrow marketplaces of the Old City of Jerusalem

O Lord, hear my prayer, give ear to my
    supplications.
In Your faithfulness answer me, in Your
    righteousness.
For the enemy is pursuing me,
he has crushed my life to the ground.
He has made me dwell in darkness,
like the dead of long ago.

My spirit faints within me,
My heart is desolate.
I remember the days of the past,
I meditate on all Your work.
I contemplate the work of Your hands.
Quickly answer me, O Lord,
My spirit is exhausted.

Hide not Your face from me or I will be
    like those who go down into the pit.
Cause me to hear Your covenant love in
    the morning,
for I have trusted in You.
Make me know the way I should walk,
for I have lifted my soul to You.

The Eighth Station: Jesus Speaks to the Women of Jerusalem

Around the corner, west on Aqabat el-Khanka Street, a round stone embedded in the wall of the Greek Monastery of St. Charambalos marks the Eighth Station, where some women wept for Jesus as he carried his cross. Letters surrounding a cross are cut into the stone: "IC XC NIKA," meaning, "Jesus Christ conquers." However, the same Chapel of the Seventh Station is where we usually recall those compassionate women.

A large number of the people followed Him, and some women were mourning and lamenting Him. Turning to them Jesus said,

Daughters of Jerusalem, do not weep for Me. Rather, weep for yourselves and for your children, for the days are coming in which they will say, "Blessed are the sterile and the wombs which did not bear and the breasts which did not nurse." Then they will begin to say to the mountains, "Fall on us!" and to the hills, "Hide us!" For if they do these things when the tree is green, what will happen when it is dry?

Let us pray.
Lord Jesus Christ, while you were suffering you showed more concern for the women of Jerusalem who would one day suffer greatly in the destruction of their city than for yourself. You were more concerned that the people harming you would later experience terrible desolation. You have redeemed us to preserve us from desolation at the Last Judgment. Amen.

Then the kings of the earth, and the great people, and the generals, the rich, the strong, and every slave and free person will hide themselves in the caves and the rocks of the mountains. They will say to the mountains and to the rocks, "Fall on us and hide us from the face of the One seated on the throne and from the wrath of the Lamb! For the great day of their wrath has come, and who will be able to stand it?"

Let us pray.
Lord Jesus, you suffered and died to give us forgiveness of our sins and redemption. Grant us true grief for our offenses and help us to mourn for the sins of the world, so we may avoid sin and recall the world from evil. Amen.

The Ninth Station: Jesus Falls a Third Time

You reach this station by walking around the Monastery of St. Charambalos and then walking south through the Suq Khan ez-Zeit. A wide stairway on the right leads up to a street, which one follows up to the entrance of the Coptic Orthodox Patriarchate. To the left of the door, a pillar embedded in the wall marks the Ninth Station; to the right there is a Coptic Orthodox chapel, where the priest may permit pilgrims to pray.

Jesus certainly experienced great weakness during his journey through Jerusalem, bearing his cross. Praying the psalms of lament are a way to express sorrow, grief, and pain within prayers inspired by the Holy Spirit. Psalm 69 is appropriate for reflecting on Christ's stumble and fall on the Via Dolorosa:

Save Me, O God, for water has reached My neck;
I have sunk in the mud of the deep, and there is no standing.
I came into the depths of water, the flood overwhelms Me.
I am wearied with calling out, My throat is parched.
My eyes fail while I wait for My God.
More numerous than the hairs of My head are those who without cause hate Me.
Powerful are those who would cut Me off, My lying enemies.
Let My prayer come to You, O Lord, in a favorable time.
O God, in the abundance of Your covenant love, answer Me in the truth of Your salvation.
Do not let the flood of water overwhelm Me; do not let the deep swallow Me;
Do not let the pit shut its mouth on Me.
Answer Me, O Lord, because Your covenant love is good.
According to the abundance of Your compassion, turn to Me.

Let us pray.
Lord Jesus Christ, you lead all humanity on the way of the cross. You, the Good Shepherd and Life itself, have laid down your life for the sake of the sheep. When you announced that "the hour has come when the Son of Man is to be glorified," you added, "Unless the grain of wheat falls into the ground and dies, it remains alone, but if it dies it bears much fruit." By your fall and your death, may you bear much fruit in us and throughout your Church. Amen.

The Holy Sepulcher Church

We enter the Holy Sepulcher Church across a courtyard and through a large, open door. Immediately upon entering, you'll see a narrow, steep stairway which leads up to Calvary.

A floor is built upon pillars to facilitate a visit to the site of Jesus's crucifixion. At the top, the rock of Calvary is protected by glass, and there are three altars. The Greek Orthodox altar is immediately in front of a large crucifix with life-size icons of the Blessed Virgin Mary and St. John on either side. You can kneel under this Greek altar, where you'll notice a metal plate with a hole in it. Through this hole you can touch the actual rock of Calvary. Usually a line of pilgrims forms so each one can

take a turn touching this holy place. It is a good opportunity to consider Jesus being stripped of his garments, being nailed to the cross (depicted in a mosaic on the wall above Calvary), the raising of Jesus on the cross, his last words, his last breath, and the grief of his Mother standing close by through it all—along with John, Mary Magdalene, Mary the sister of Jesus's Mother and the wife of Clopas, Joseph of Arimathea, and Nicodemus.

When the soldiers crucified Jesus, they took His garments and made four pieces, one piece for each soldier. The tunic was seamless, woven from the top throughout the whole. Therefore they said to each other, "Let us not cut it but let us cast lots for it." This was so that the Scripture might be fulfilled: "They divided my garments among them and for my cloak they have cast lots." Therefore the soldiers did these things.

Once again the Roman soldiers, ignorant of Scripture, fulfill a prophecy from the Psalms that they would "divide my garments and cast lots for my clothes." While the process of Jesus's suffering, crucifixion, and death seemed in the control of its perpetrators, in fact it was under God's control. His prophets had foretold these things, and various people, including those completely ignorant of Scripture, took roles in their fulfillment.

Let us pray.
Lord, we are often so confused by the tragic events of our lives and of the world around us. We sometimes fear that this is all out of your control, and we are confused. Bring to our minds these events of your most painful death so that we may understand how they were part of God's plan from the beginning. May we remember that when life seems disordered, chaotic, and even meaningless, we can still turn to you and your Providence. We may not see what you are doing until long after the difficult events pass us by, yet we will learn from your passion and death that all things can work out to the good—only, we must love you through it all. Amen.

The Crucifixion of Jesus

When they came to the place called "Golgotha," which means "Skull Place," they gave Him wine mixed with gall to drink. But on tasting it, He did not want to drink it.

The people passing Him by blasphemed Him, shaking their heads and saying, "He is the one who would destroy the Temple and in three days build it! Save Yourself, if You are the Son of God! Come down from the cross!"

Likewise, the chief priests mocked Him, along with the scribes and elders, saying, "Others He saved; Himself He cannot save! He is the King of Israel; let Him come down now from the cross and we will believe in Him! He trusted in God, let Him save Him now if He wants Him!"

The thieves crucified with Him taunted Him in the same way. Jesus said, "Father, forgive them, for they do not know what they are doing."

Then he said, "Jesus, remember me when You come into Your kingdom."

He said to him, "Amen I say to you, today you will be with Me in Paradise."

Pilate wrote an inscription and placed it on the cross. It read, "Jesus the Nazorean, King of the Jews." Therefore many read this inscription because the place where Jesus was crucified was near the city, and it was written in Hebrew, Latin and Greek. Therefore the high priests said to Pilate, "Do not write 'The King of the Jews,' but that he said, 'I am the King of the Jews.'" Pilate answered, "What I have written, I have written."

Let us pray.
Lord Jesus, from the cross you offered the most powerful forgiveness. Not only did you ask the heavenly Father to forgive those who mocked and tormented you, you even gave an excuse for their behavior—"They do not know what they are doing." I do not understand my sins either. I am bewildered by my confusion of good intentions and bad motives. Intercede for me with the same tender prayer so that our heavenly Father may forgive me, too. Let me steal a promise of being with you in paradise, like that greatest of all good thieves who stole salvation by faith in you at the very end of his life. May I accept you as my true King now and forever. Amen.

Jesus Dies on the Cross

Meditating on the Greek altar before the life-size crucifix and icons of the Blessed Mother and St. John, we recall the four final sayings of Jesus and his last breath.

Near Jesus's cross stood His Mother, Mary the wife of Clopas, and Mary Magdalene. Upon seeing His Mother and the disciple whom he loved, He said to His Mother, "Woman, behold your son." Then He said to the disciple, "Behold your Mother." And from that hour the disciple took her into his care.

At noon darkness came upon the whole earth until three. Around three Jesus cried aloud, "Eli, Eli, lema sabachthani?" That is, "My God, My God, why have You forsaken Me?"

Knowing that all was accomplished, so that Scripture might be fulfilled, Jesus said, "I thirst." A vessel full of sour wine was nearby, so a sponge full of the sour wine was put on hyssop and brought near to His mouth. When He took the wine Jesus said, "It is finished." Dropping His head He gave up the Spirit.

The sun darkened and the curtain of the Temple was split in the middle. Jesus said in a loud voice, "Father, into Your hands I commend My Spirit." Having said this, He expired.

When the centurion and Jesus's guards saw the earthquake and what had happened, they were very frightened. They said, "Truly, this one was a Son of God!"

The soldiers broke the legs of the two men crucified with him. Seeing that Jesus was already dead, they did not break his legs. Instead, a soldier pierced his side with a lance. Immediately blood and water came out. The one who saw it has testified and his testimony is true. This happened to fulfill the Scripture, "They did not break his bones." Another Scripture says, "They have looked upon him whom they pierced."

Even at the very end, the Roman soldiers, who knew nothing of the Old Testament prophecies, became the instruments to fulfill them. By not breaking Jesus's legs, as they had done to the thieves to hasten their deaths, the soldiers kept the Old Testament law that prohibited breaking any bones of the Passover lamb. The Lamb of God did not have his bones broken either. Also, Zechariah describes the Lord speaking, saying, "They shall look upon me whom they pierced." The Hebrew is shocking—how can they possibly pierce God's side? Yet here on the cross the pagan Roman soldiers do just that and unwittingly fulfill a prophecy.

Let us pray.

Lord, from the cross you continue to give to us great gifts through your simple words. You make your Mother the Mother of the beloved disciple—not only John, but every beloved disciple. May we always cherish her love and care and show ourselves worthy of your gift. You thirsted, Lord Jesus. You thirst for our souls and for the souls of every sinner in the world. May we slake your thirst by always drawing close to you and by bringing many others to come to know you as Lord and Savior.

You commended your spirit into the Father's hands as you were dying on the cross. May we, like St. Stephen the Deacon, the first martyr, also commend our lives into your hands, most especially at the hour of our death. You have won the grace of dying well for us; we seek this grace at every moment that we must die to ourselves, and especially when it comes time to breathe our last.

Holy Savior Jesus, you taught that when you would be lifted from the earth you would draw all men to yourself. Let us trust this wisdom about the cross and never shrink away from proclaiming it to all people. May we honor your cross, mourn your death, and have absolute confidence in its power to forgive the sins of the world, for you are Lord forever and ever. Amen.

The Stone of the Anointing

The Altar of the Sorrowful Mother and the Stone of the Anointing

The small Altar of the Sorrowful Mother, with a sixteenth-century image of Our Lady of Sorrows donated in 1778 by Maria I of Braganza, Queen of Portugal, marks where Mary received Jesus's body into her arms after he was taken down from the cross. Upon descending Calvary, you can also pray at the Stone of the Anointing, a ninth-century memorial of the preparation of Jesus's body for burial with spices. On the wall behind the Stone of the Anointing is a Greek mosaic icon depicting the removal of Jesus's body from the cross, the anointing of his body, and his burial.

The evening of the Preparation Day, which is the day before the Sabbath, was approaching. Joseph of Arimathea boldly went to Pilate and asked for the body of Jesus.

Pilate was amazed that He had already died. He summoned the centurion to ask if indeed He had died. When he knew it from the centurion, he gave the corpse to Joseph.

Joseph bought a linen and took Him down to wrap Him in the linen.

Then Nicodemus brought a mixture of myrrh and aloes weighing a hundred pounds. They took Jesus's body and bound it in linen with the spices, as is the burial custom of the Jews.

Let us pray.
Lord, we are a confusion of attitudes toward you, like Joseph and Nicodemus. At times we hide our faith and love like cowards, keeping your words in the dark. Other times we love boldly. Transform us into bold believers and lovers, caring for you in the poor and needy. Amen.

Mosaic of Jesus's burial in the tomb

At the Tomb

A visit to the tomb of Jesus evokes wonder. Silent awe is appropriate as we consider Christ's silence in the dark, stone-enclosed tomb. Typically pilgrims wait in line to visit inside the tomb, and too many chat idly while they do so. A better consideration is the quiet grief of the Blessed Mother, the preparations by the holy women disciples, and their need to leave him in the tomb until after the Sabbath was over. Just as God rested on the first Sabbath, so did he rest on this particular Sabbath after having redeemed the world by his death on the cross.

The tomb of Jesus is not far from Mount Calvary, which is as St. John described it: "There was in the place where he was crucified a garden and in the garden a new tomb in which no one had ever been laid." After entering the Holy Sepulcher Church, a short walk to the left and around a corner brings us to the edicule built over the remains of the tomb. Visitors are welcome for just a short visit, since so many pilgrims come primarily to see this sacred spot. In the middle of the first room, known as the Chapel of the Angels, you'll notice a pillar with a square stone on top. This is the last surviving fragment of the rolling stone that had been placed before the original tomb. A smaller doorway leads into the tomb. The place where Jesus was laid is covered by a slab of marble.

Just north of the tomb, on the Franciscan side, is the Altar of St. Mary Magdalene, built next to a large pillar. This area commemorates the appearance of Jesus to Mary Magdalene after his resurrection. A large bronze bas-relief of Jesus meeting St. Mary Magdalene is above the altar; across from it is a painting of Christ meeting her dressed as a gardener.

They placed him in a tomb which was hewn from rock. Then Joseph rolled a stone against the entrance of the tomb. Mary Magdalene and Mary the Mother of Joses observed where He had been laid.

He Is Risen!

On the first day of the week, Mary Magdalene came to the tomb at dawn, while it was still dark, and saw that the stone was removed from the tomb. Then she ran and went to Simon Peter and to the other disciple whom Jesus loved, and said, "They have taken the Lord from the tomb and we do not know where they have put Him!"

Peter and the other disciple went out and came to the tomb. The two ran together but the other disciple ran ahead, faster than Peter, and he came to the tomb first. Then bending down, he saw the linen cloth set in place; however he did not enter. Then Simon Peter came following him, entered the tomb, and saw the linens set in place. The cloth which was on His head was not placed with the linen cloth but was rolled up in another place. Then the other disciple, who first had come to the tomb, saw and believed. For He did not yet understand the Scripture, that it was necessary for Him to rise from the dead. Then the disciples went home again.

Mary stood outside the tomb crying. Then, as she was crying, she bent over into the tomb and saw two angels in white seated, one at the head and one at the foot, where the Body of Jesus had been placed. Then they said to her, "Woman, why are you crying?"

She said to them, "Because they have taken away my Lord and I know not where they have put Him!" Having said these things, she turned around and saw Jesus standing there, but she did not know that it was Jesus.

Jesus said to her, "Woman, why are you crying? Whom do you seek?"

Thinking he was the gardener, she said to Him, "Sir, if You have carried Him away, tell me where You have put Him and I will take Him."

Jesus said, "Mary!"

Turning, she said, "Rabbouni!" This means, "Teacher!"

Jesus said to her, "Do not cling to Me, for I have not yet ascended to My Father. Go to My brothers and tell them, 'I am ascending to My Father and your Father, to My God and your God.'"

Mary Magdalene went and announced to the disciples that she had seen the Lord and the things He said to her.

A characteristic of each of the stories of the Resurrection is that they all entail having faith in the reality of Jesus risen from the dead. Mary Magdalene and the other women came to the tomb expecting to anoint a corpse. Then, when she discovered the empty tomb, she assumed that someone had stolen the body, and she ran to the apostles with this tragic news. Even when she saw Jesus himself, she assumed he was the gardener and asked where he took

the body. The personal encounter in which the Risen Lord Jesus pronounces her name is finally the moment of conversion. This pattern of unbelief followed by conversion applies to the other appearances of Jesus to the disciples at Emmaus and the apostles in the Upper Room.

Our faith in Jesus's Resurrection distinguishes the Christian faith from mere philosophies. God has acted more powerfully than philosophers can think he would, by overcoming sin and death through the death and Resurrection of Jesus Christ. Let us take this Good News into a world of cynicism and futility in order to proclaim a hope based, not only on what God has done in Jesus Christ's Resurrection, but also on a similar resurrection in store for those who believe in Christ and live as he did.

Let us pray.
Lord, we praise you for rising from the dead. You give us the anchor of hope for our own resurrection by rising from this tomb. Make us evangelists of this Good News to the world, as you were with St. Mary Magdalene. May we faithfully tell the hopeless that you are their hope, you who are our glory and our life. Amen.

The Chapel Commemorating the Risen Christ's Appearance to the Blessed Virgin Mary

This event of Christ's appearance to his Mother after his Resurrection is not recorded in sacred Scripture, but it may be presumed since the Blessed Virgin Mary joined the apostles in prayer after the Ascension of Jesus Christ. The Franciscans have custody of this chapel, and Catholics may celebrate Holy Mass here or pray before the Blessed Sacrament, which is reserved in the tabernacle. An appropriate prayer or hymn is the *Regina Caeli*.

Let us pray.
Queen of heaven rejoice, Alleluia!
For he whom you merited to bear, Alleluia!
Has risen as he said, Alleluia!
Rejoice and be glad, O Virgin Mary, Alleluia!
For the Lord has truly risen, Alleluia!
O God, who by the resurrection of your Son, our Lord Jesus Christ, has vouchsafed to make glad the whole world: grant, we beseech you, through the intercession of the Virgin Mary, his Mother, we may lay hold of the joys of eternal life. Through the same Christ our Lord. Amen.

The Temple Mount

The Temple Mount, today known as the Haram esh-Sharif, meaning "the Noble Enclosure," covers about 135 acres. Gardens and courtyards surround two mosques: the Dome of the Rock and the Al Aqsa. The Dome of the Rock, built between A.D. 688 and 691, is an exquisite building of tiles, mosaics, and a roof recovered with gold in 1994 by King Hussein. The Al Aqsa (meaning "the Furthermost") commemorates Mohammed's night journey to heaven. In biblical times this place was the Temple Mount, where Solomon built the First Temple, Zerubbabel built the Second Temple, and Herod reconstructed the Second Temple. Surrounding the Mount is a retaining wall built by Herod made of very large

stone blocks, a section of which forms the holiest shrine in Judaism—the Western Wall, or Kotel.

Since the Jerusalem temple figures so prominently in both the Old and New Testaments, there is much for us to contemplate from many parts of the Bible. However, it is not permitted for non-Muslims to pray publicly on the Mount, and these wishes must be respected. Similarly, Jewish people pray at the Western Wall, the Kotel, and they must also be respected in their most sacred place of worship. The best place for Christians to pray together is in the Archaeological Garden south of the Temple Mount, particularly on the steps to the Temple that Herod the Great had built.

The Old Testament identifies the site of the Temple as Mount Moriah, where Abraham took Isaac to be sacrificed. The Lord stopped Abraham, and a ram was sacrificed instead. This connects Abraham, the great ancestor of Israel, with the one place in the world where Israel can offer sacrifices to God. The importance of sacrificial worship began at the earliest stages of the Old Testament, and it continued in Israel until the destruction of the Temple in A.D. 70. Christianity does not require any animal sacrifices, but Christ's death and the Eucharist he established are understood as the sacrifice that replaces the Old Testament rituals. The Temple Mount connects us with a history of worship, prayer, and sacrifice that extends back to Abraham, but the Christian faith holds that God is now worshiped throughout the world by the sacrifice of his Son, Jesus Christ.

When David wanted to build a house for the Lord, that is, a temple, God said no. In First Chronicles, David explains to Solomon the Lord's reason to prohibit David from building the house: "You have shed much blood and made great wars, so you will not build a house for My Name." Solomon, whose name means "peace," would build the Temple.

However, the Lord did promise to build David's "house," that is, his dynasty, forever. In fact, David's dynasty ruled for over four hundred years, longer than the dynasties of Egypt, Assyria, or Babylon. Yet, in 587 B.C. the Babylonians destroyed Jerusalem and took the king captive, thereby ending the earthly dynasty. Still, from David's family would come the Messiah, as the prophets foretold. God's promise to build David's family has become more relevant to us than Solomon's building the Temple. It is precisely because Jesus Christ is God and man, Son of David and Son of God, that he fulfills the promise for a son to sit on David's throne forever.

Solomon Builds the Temple and Dedicates It

The Bible gives two long accounts of the building and dedication of the Temple by Solomon. First, King Solomon purchased cedar from King Hiram of Tyre and conscripted thousands of Israelite laborers to quarry blocks of stone. Workers paneled the walls with cedar and covered them with much gold, precious stones, and cloth. They made the sacred vessels of bronze. The building was begun in the early 960s B.C. and was completed in seven years. Solomon then dedicated the Temple with many sacrifices, musical accompaniment, and the following prayer:

Blessed be the Lord the God of Israel, who spoke by His mouth to David my father and by His hand has fulfilled it.

Now the Lord has established His word, which He spoke. I am established after David my father and sit on the throne of Israel. As the Lord spoke, I built the house to the Name of the Lord, the God of Israel. I made a place for the Ark of the Covenant of the Lord, which he made with our fathers when He brought them from the land of Egypt.

Indeed, is it possible that God dwells on earth? Behold, heaven, even highest heaven cannot contain You; how can this house which I have built? So turn to Your servant's prayer and supplications, Lord my God, to hear the praise and prayer which Your servant prays before You today.

Let Your eyes be opened to this house night and day, to the place of which You have said, "My Name is there to listen to the prayer which My servant will pray in this place."

You will hear the supplications of Your servant and Your people Israel, which they address to this place. You will listen in Your dwelling place in heaven. You will listen and forgive.

Let us pray.
Lord, we believe that you still hear us, night and day, and will answer our needs. We no longer can pray in Solomon's Temple, but we believe that you hear our prayer in any place from which we call upon you. Dwell within our hearts so that we might one day dwell within your temple in heaven, where we will worship you night and day, face-to-face, without ceasing for all eternity. Amen.

The Destruction of the Temple

The Archaeological Garden south of the Temple Mount, near the Dung Gate, contains Second Temple ruins. At the southwest corner of the Temple, where many fallen stones lie about, we can consider and pray over the Temple's fall. The Temple was destroyed twice and desecrated various times. The Babylonians destroyed it in July 587 B.C. The Greek king of Syria, Antiochus IV Epiphanes, desecrated it in 168 B.C. Then, in A.D. 70, the Romans destroyed the Temple that had been rebuilt by Herod the Great.

Let us pray.
Lord, these ruins remind us of the desolation that results from breaking your covenant. By your grace keep us faithful to your new covenant and protect us from the destruction of our souls in hell. We ask this through Jesus Christ our Lord. Amen.

In the Archaeological Park, outside the wall, is the stairway of the "Hulda Gate," which had been built by Herod the Great as the entrance to the Temple. The New Testament personages entered the Temple through this gate, so it is an excellent place to consider the New Testament passages relating to the Temple.

The Annunciation of John the Baptist's Birth

In the days of Herod, the king of Judea, there was a priest named Zechariah, of the priestly division of Abijah. His wife was from the daughters of Aaron, and her name was Elizabeth. Both of them were righteous before God, walking blamelessly in all the commandments and ordinances of the Lord. But they had no child, since Elizabeth was sterile, and both were advanced in age.

While he was exercising priestly ministry before God, according to the order of his priestly division, as was the custom of the priestly ministry, it fell by lot that he would go into the Temple of the Lord to offer incense. The whole multitude of the people was outside at the hour of the incense.

Then an angel of the Lord appeared to him, standing at the right of the altar of incense. Zechariah was troubled and fear fell upon him. But the angel said to him, "Fear not, Zechariah, for your prayer has been heard. Your wife will bear you a son and you will name him John. You will have joy and be glad, indeed, many will rejoice at his birth. For he will be great before the Lord. He will not drink wine or strong drink, but he will be filled with the Holy Spirit, even from his mother's womb. He will turn many of the children of Israel to the Lord their God. He will go before him in the spirit and power of Elijah, to turn the hearts of fathers to the children and the disobedient to the understanding of the righteous, to prepare for the Lord a people well equipped."

Then Zechariah said to the angel, "How will I know this? I am old and my wife is advanced in her days."

The angel answered him, "I am Gabriel, who stands before God. I was sent to speak to you and announce to you these good tidings. Now see, you will be mute and unable to speak until the days when these things happen. This is because you did not believe my words, which will be fulfilled in their time."

The people were waiting, amazed at how long he was in the Temple. When he came out unable to speak, they realized that he had seen a vision in the Temple. He kept making signs to them and remained mute. When the days of his service were completed, he returned to his home. After these days, Elizabeth his wife conceived. She kept herself in seclusion for five months, saying, "Thus has the Lord acted in the days in which He showed concern to remove my reproach among men."

Zechariah was chosen by lot in his old age to offer the incense in the Temple. The first book of Chronicles describes the twenty-four divisions of priests who served in the Temple, with many individuals in each division. This made it unlikely that any individual would offer the incense more than once. While Zechariah was exercising this privilege, God sent the angel Gabriel. He announced to Zechariah the birth of John the Baptist, who will go before the Lord and turn people to God, in fulfillment of the prophecies in Malachi 3:1 and 4:5–6. He will have the spirit and power of Elijah in preparation for the Messiah as well as the power of the Holy Spirit from the womb.

Zechariah's response was, "How will I know this?" He wanted proof that the angel's words were true because his focus on his wife's advanced age made this promise seem impossible. His lack of faith did not take away the promise, but he would be punished with silence until its fulfillment at John's birth. He then had enough faith to return home and beget John, and his wife Elizabeth was filled with amazement at what had taken place within her womb.

The Purification of the Blessed Virgin Mary and the Presentation of Jesus

Just south of the Herodian entrance to the Temple can be found ancient miqvahs, which are baths for ritual purification, according to Jewish Law. Childbirth was one of the times when such purification was necessary. In addition, since Jesus was Mary's firstborn son, it was necessary to offer a sacrifice to redeem Him.

When the days of their purification were fulfilled according to the Law of Moses, they brought Him to Jerusalem to present Him to the Lord. As it is written in the Law of the Lord, "Every male that opens the womb will be called holy to the Lord." They brought a sacrifice according to what is said in the Law of the Lord, "A pair of pigeons or two turtledoves."

There was a man in Jerusalem named Simeon. He was a righteous and pious man, awaiting the consolation of Israel, and the Holy Spirit was on him. It had been revealed to him by the Holy Spirit that he would not see death before he saw the Christ of the Lord. He came into the Temple by the Spirit as the parents were bringing the boy Jesus to do what was customary by law for him. Then Simeon received Him into his arms, blessed God and said, "Now you may dismiss your servant in peace Lord, according to Your word. For my eyes have seen Your salvation which You have prepared before all the peoples. A light for the revelation of the gentiles and the glory of Your people Israel."

His father and mother were amazed at what was being said about Him.

Then Simeon blessed them and said to Mary His Mother, "Behold, He is set for the fall and the rise of many in Israel and as a sign of contradiction. A sword will pierce your soul so that the thoughts of many hearts might be revealed."

Now Anna was a prophet, the daughter of Phanuel, from the tribe of Asher. She was advanced in age, having lived with her husband for seven years after having been a virgin, and she was a widow for eighty-four years. She did not cease offering fasting and prayers in the Temple day and night. At that hour she stood nearby. She thanked God and spoke about Him to everyone who was awaiting the redemption of Israel.

When they had finished everything according to the Law of the Lord, they returned to Galilee, to their own city of Nazareth. The child grew and became strong, filled with wisdom and the grace of God was with Him.

Presentation of Jesus in the Temple, *by Hans Holbein*

This scene is occasioned by Joseph and Mary fulfilling the Law of the firstborn son. St. Paul reflects on the importance of this obedience to the Law: "When the fullness of time had come, God sent His Son, born of a woman, born under the Law that he might redeem those under the Law, so that we might receive adoption as sons."

This obedience becomes the occasion for the movement of the Holy Spirit, who led Simeon and Anna into the temple to give witness to this child. The Holy Spirit inspired Simeon to proclaim that he could die in peace because he had seen the salvation God prepared in the Infant Jesus for Israel and the whole world. He also addressed two statements to Mary, which is exceptional, since normally such a word would be addressed to the father. The first concerns Jesus, as the one set for the rise and fall of many in Israel. One can read Luke and the other Gospels in light of this saying, as various people rise in healing, forgiveness, and peace through their encounters with Jesus, while others lack faith in him and ultimately fall.

Simeon's second statement concerns Mary: A sword will pierce her heart so that the inner thoughts of many might be revealed. She will suffer to the very core because she has borne Jesus, but this suffering is not only for her, it is for her to give insight to other people. They can come to deeper understanding of themselves and of God through the pain Mary undergoes in relation to Jesus. This mystery has become part of the Church's reflection on the importance of Mary in everyone's spiritual life.

Let us pray.

Dear Blessed Mother Mary, you suffered in various ways precisely because you loved Jesus and obeyed God. We come to you in your sorrows, especially as you stood at the cross of Jesus, and ask you to help us gain wisdom about our own suffering, difficulties, and challenges of life. Keep us always faithful to God, even as you were. May our lives become one with your willingness to proclaim, "Let it be according to God's word." Amen.

The Finding of the Child Jesus in the Temple

As was the custom, his parents used to go to Jerusalem for the feast of Passover. When he was twelve years old, they went up according to the custom of the feast. When the days were completed, and they returned, the boy Jesus remained in Jerusalem, though his parents did not know it. Thinking he was in the caravan, they went a day's journey. They sought him among the relatives and acquaintances, and when they did not find him they returned to Jerusalem seeking him. After three days they found him in the Temple, seated among the teachers, listening to them and asking them questions. All who heard him were amazed at his understanding and answers.

When his parents saw him, they were amazed, and his Mother said to him, "Son, why have you done this to us? See, your father and I are deeply distressed looking for you."

He said to them, "Why were you looking for me? Did you not know that it was necessary for me to be about my Father's business?"

They did not understand the word which he had spoken to them. He went down with them and came to Nazareth, and He was subject to them. His Mother kept all these words in her heart. And Jesus advanced in wisdom, age and grace before God and men.

We can consider a number of elements in this episode. First, the Holy Family lived out the Law of Moses, which required Israel to assemble in Jerusalem three times a year for the great feasts: Passover, Pentecost, and Tabernacles. St. Luke mentions that it was their custom "every year" to join hundreds of thousands of fellow Jews on pilgrimage to this festival.

Second, St. Luke mentions this particular occasion because of the unusual occurrence of Jesus staying behind in Jerusalem. Jesus remained calmly in his Father's house. This indicates his awareness of being God's Son. The holiness of Mary and Joseph did not always give them clarity about Jesus's words and deeds; they remained a mystery to be pondered deeply throughout the silent years in Nazareth. We can learn from this about our own need to contemplate the mysteries of the faith, letting them deepen over many years to gain proper perspective on how and why God acts the way he does with us.

Third, Jesus continued to grow in wisdom, age, and grace throughout the following years. The great mystery is that Jesus spent thirty years obeying two humans, three years teaching his disciples, and three hours redeeming the world. Perhaps this can help us appreciate the ordinariness of our lives more fully.

Jesus Cleanses the Temple

The Passover of the Jews was near, and Jesus went up to Jerusalem. He found people selling oxen, sheep and doves, and people seated changing coins. After making a whip from ropes, he expelled them all from the Temple, along with the sheep and oxen. He spilled out the coins of the money changers and overturned the tables. To those selling doves He said, "Take these things away from here; do not make my Father's House a marketplace!" His disciples remembered that it is written, "Zeal for Your House has consumed me" [Psalm 69:9].

Therefore the Jewish people answered Him: "What sign do You show us that we may believe?"

Jesus answered them, "Destroy this Temple and in three days I will raise it up."

Therefore the Jews said, "This Temple was built in forty-six years, and You would raise it up in three days?" He was speaking about the temple of his body.

Therefore, when he was raised from the dead, his disciples remembered that he had said this, and they believed in the Scripture and in the word which Jesus had said.

This passage indicates that the Temple had been under Herod's reconstruction for forty-six years already. That would place this event in A.D. 27, which was a Jewish Jubilee year, based on calculations from Ezekiel 40:1, which mentions a Jubilee year in 573 B.C. Jesus began his public ministry during a Jubilee as a way to indicate that his whole mission is to bring the release, healing, and reconciliation he announced in reading from the book of Isaiah.

Jesus was present in the Temple for the Passover, the first of three Passovers mentioned in John's Gospel. As when he was twelve, he looked upon the Temple as his own Father's house and therefore treated the selling and money changing quite harshly, taking them as a personal offense. The rest of the people asked Jesus for a sign to believe that he had the authority to take so much charge over the Temple. When he promised to raise up "this temple" in three days after they would destroy it, they thought immediately of the building that Herod had constructed. It was extremely beautiful and costly, so they could not understand the sign he was giving them. The disciples probably did not understand it any better at that point either, but Jesus's Resurrection gave his saying a new meaning. They could see the sign in his death and Resurrection, and for that reason Thomas would declare, "My Lord and my God!" to the Risen Jesus. It would then make sense to them that the Temple of God was truly the house of Jesus's Father.

Christ Driving the Traders from the Temple, *by El Greco*

Let us pray.

Lord Jesus, we have introduced so many practices and actions into our lives that are incompatible with the holiness to which you call us. You want our bodies to become the temples of the Holy Spirit, but we bring in our selfishness, deceits, greed, lusts, and lack of faith to mar the beauty you intend our lives to have. We ask you to enter our lives again and cleanse us. May we confess our sins and let you remove all that is inconsistent with the life to which you call us. Grant us a zeal for you and your truth.

Lord Jesus, we also remember that you laid down your life and in three days you rose from the dead in fulfillment of the Scriptures. You have become the cornerstone of the Church; everything rests on you. Grant us deeper faith in the Sscriptures and in your Word so that we may continue to build upon you, who are Lord forever and ever. Amen.

MOUNT OF OLIVES

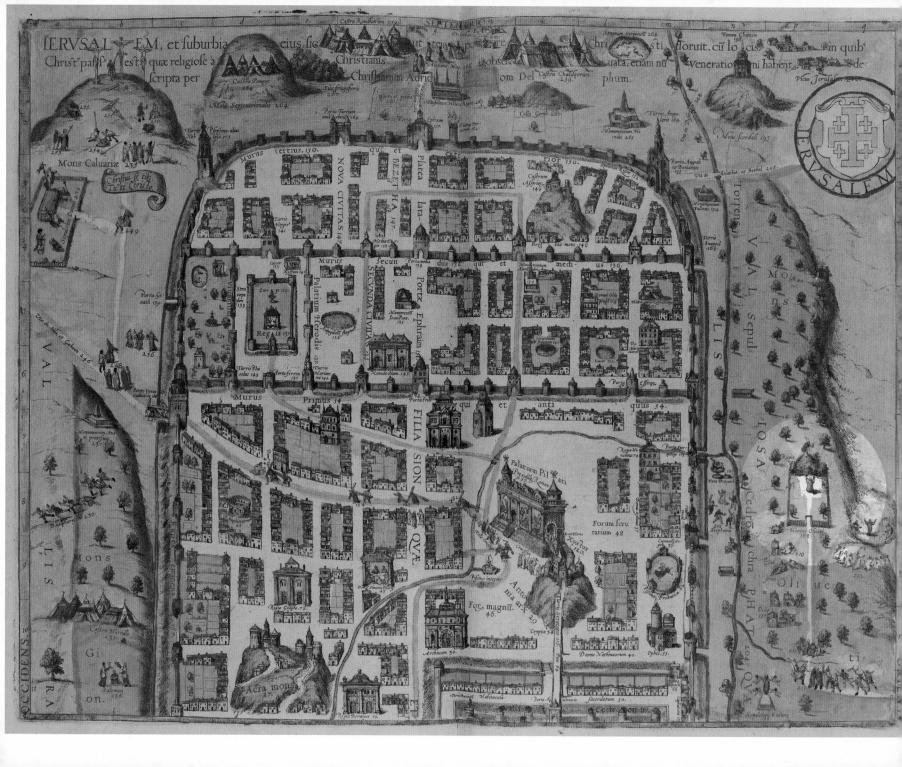

The Ascension Chapel

At the highest point of the Mount of Olives is a twelfth-century, octagonal Crusader chapel. Originally it stood open to the sky, without a roof, to indicate the Lord's Ascension into heaven. Inside the chapel, on the floor, a rectangle of bedrock is exposed, surrounded by a rectangle of marble. In the rock you can make out the shape of a footprint that, according to tradition, marks the spot from which Jesus ascended into heaven.

After the Crusades, the Muslims built a mosque next to the chapel, and they now possess the property. However, pilgrims are permitted to pray here on any day, and Mass

According to tradition, this shape of a footprint in the bedrock marks the site where Christ ascended into heaven

is celebrated here on Ascension Thursday, both by the Gregorian calendar used by Catholics and the Julian calendar used by the Orthodox. In fact, you can see iron hooks embedded in the walls surrounding the chapel. These are for tents set up on Ascension Thursday to make possible multiple Masses both inside and outside the chapel.

Jesus presented himself alive with many proofs to the apostles after he had suffered, appearing to them for forty days and speaking about the kingdom of God. Having eaten with them, he ordered them not to leave Jerusalem but to "wait for the promise of the Father, of which you have heard from me. John baptized with water, but you will be baptized by the Holy Spirit not many days from now."

Then those who were assembled asked him, "Lord, is it at this time that you will restore the Kingdom to Israel?"

He said to them,

"It is not for you to know the times or the seasons which the Father has set by his own authority. However, you will receive the power of the Holy Spirit coming upon you and you will be my witnesses in Jerusalem and in all Judea and Samaria and until the ends of the earth."

And when he had said these things they saw him lifted up and a cloud took him up from their eyes. And as they were staring intently into the sky where he had gone, behold, two men dressed in white clothing stood before them. They said, "Galilean Men, why do you stand looking into the sky? This Jesus who was taken up from you into heaven will return just as you saw him go into the sky!"

Then they returned to Jerusalem from the Mount called Olives, which is near Jerusalem, about a Sabbath day's journey.

At other sites we consider that Jesus experienced great depths of sorrow and pain—Gethsemane where he sweat blood, Caiaphas's house where he was condemned and sat in a pitch-dark pit, Pilate's court where the cross was placed upon him, and finally Calvary where he died. However, here on the Mount of Olives Jesus went to the heights, from the top of the highest hill in Jerusalem up to heaven itself.

An iron hook in the wall of Ascension Chapel

In Acts, Luke summarizes Jesus's teaching during the forty days after Easter to show that Jesus taught in continuity with his message about the kingdom during his whole public ministry. This is true of Jesus's promise that his disciples would be baptized in the Holy Spirit, as John the Baptist had said, except that Jesus here let them know that the Holy Spirit would come in a few days. When the disciples tried to determine the timing of the restoration of the kingdom, Jesus again taught that this is not for them to know. Later they would accept their ignorance of such things and teach the other churches that the day of Christ's judgment is unknown and will come like a thief in the night. Therefore, the two important things for them to know, they realized, are that the Holy Spirit was about to come upon them soon and that they would give testimony to Jesus, spreading out from Jerusalem to Judea, Samaria, and the ends of the world. This verse helps form the structure of the Acts of the Apostles as the apostles make geographic advancements in spreading the Gospel of Christ in precisely those stages.

The event of the Ascension is described quickly, simply, and soberly, as is true of Jesus's conception, birth, and resurrection. The fact of ascending is just stated. Luke writes in more detail about the apostles' staring after Jesus and the need for two angels in white to explain that they will not see him again until the end of the world. Only then do they return to Jerusalem to pray for the next nine days for the coming of the Holy Spirit—the Church's first novena, and the event that inspired the choice of nine-day periods for prayer, especially for intercession.

A number of biblical texts have helped Christians through the centuries to better understand the meaning of our Lord's ascension. First, we can look at two sections of Psalm 68:

Let God arise, let his enemies be scattered, and let those who hate him flee his face.

As smoke is driven about, drive them out;

As wax melts before fire, let the wicked be destroyed before God.

But the righteous will be glad, they will exult before God and will rejoice with gladness.

Sing to God, play music to his Name, exalt the one who rides on the clouds,

Whose name is the Lord! Exult before him! You have ascended to the heights, you have taken captive captivity.

You have received gifts among men, even the rebellious, for the Lord God to dwell there.

The relevant lines in the first strophe are "Let God arise," seen as a reference both to the Resurrection and the Ascension. This is portrayed as God's victory and the defeat of his wicked enemies. The second strophe speaks of the Lord riding on the clouds, which is usually connected with the mention of the clouds that hide Jesus from sight in the Ascension. Ephesians

quotes the third strophe's mention of "gifts among men" as a way to link the Ascension with the Lord's distribution of his gifts at Pentecost.

God is rich in mercy. Because of his great love, with which he has loved us, we were made alive in Christ, when we were dead in trespasses. By grace you were saved. He raised us and sat us in the heavens in Christ Jesus so as to show in the coming ages the excelling riches of his grace in the kindness toward us in Christ Jesus.

God's merciful love makes us alive in Christ by grace, a free gift from God. This gracious love unites us with Christ. Therefore, the purpose of the Ascension is to raise all of us in Christ and to seat us in heaven, which has been accomplished by Christ already. For that reason another passage explains that the Christian's true citizenship is in heaven:

The interior dome of Ascension Chapel

If then you have been raised with Christ, seek the things that are above, where Christ is, seated at the right hand of God. Set your minds on things that are above, not on things that are on earth. For you have died, and your life is hid with Christ in God.

Being united to Jesus Christ already gives us a share in heaven. So each Christian does well to keep a focus on the things of heaven—that is, the holiness, goodness, and virtue that belong to the life of heaven. This does not mean that one neglects or ignores the things of earth, since we all still live in this life. However, union with the ascended Jesus helps us put the things of earth in a proper perspective. Too often the earthly things demand our whole effort, and they induce us to forget holiness and virtue. Our union with Christ Jesus is an antidote to that distortion.

Grace was given to each one of us according to the measure of the gift in Christ Jesus. Therefore he says, "Having ascended into the heights, he took captive captivity and gave gifts to people." Who is the One who ascended except the one who has descended into the lower parts of the earth? The one who has descended is the one who has ascended above all the heavens so as to fill everything. He has appointed apostles, prophets, evangelists, pastors and teachers for the equipping of the saints, for the work of service, for the building of the Body of Christ, until all attain the unity of the faith and the knowledge of the Son of God into the complete man, in the measure of the stature of the fullness of Christ.

Before ascending into heaven, Jesus instructed the disciples to pray for the power of the Holy Spirit. This power includes various gifts given to each Christian, some of which are listed here. Ephesians connects the Ascension directly to the bestowal of the gifts, yet, the passage also makes the point that the ascended Christ pours out these gifts "for the work of service" and to build up the Body of Christ, the Church, until every member attains the "stature of the fullness of Christ." Jesus is not only the giver of gifts but also the norm toward whom the gifts are oriented. He is truly the "Alpha and the Omega, the first and the last, the beginning and the end" of the gifts of the Holy Spirit. Therefore, each Christian should wait to receive these gifts, though not for his or her own aggrandizement. Rather, we receive them to serve as Jesus served and to let the Holy Spirit form us into a new identity in Christ Jesus, and to help form others into this same identity in Christ Jesus.

Let us pray.
Lord Jesus, Son of God and High Priest according to the order of Melchizedek, you have ascended to the right hand of the Father as our one, true High Priest. You offer yourself perpetually to your Father as an eternal offering to take away our sins and to reconcile us sinners to God. Give us your grace to place complete hope in you, so that you may draw us up to heaven's heights after you. Throughout our life on earth, intercede for us to receive the Holy Spirit and, by his power, to receive the gifts we need to serve you and build up your Church. Send us to the ends of the earth, and may our whole lives be an offering to you for your greater glory. Amen.

Church of Pater Noster

From the third century A.D., Christians identified the cave near the place of the Ascension as a location where Jesus Christ taught his disciples. For that reason St. Helena had the Church of the Eleona (Olives) built on this spot, and in 1910 Byzantine foundations were discovered. One striking feature of this site is that the walls are covered with ceramic tiles containing the Our Father in dozens of languages. The oldest and largest plaques include a variety of European and Middle Eastern languages. This site, particularly the small cave, is associated with two episodes from the Gospels: Nicodemus's night visit and the teaching of the Our Father.

CHAPTER TEN

Nicodemus Visits Jesus

There was a man from the Pharisees, Nicodemus by name, who was a leader of the Judeans. He came to Jesus by night and said to him, "Rabbi, we know that you are a teacher who has come from God, for no one is able to do the signs which you do unless God is with him."

Jesus said to him, "Amen, amen I say to you, unless someone is born again, he is not able to see the Kingdom of God."

Nicodemus said to him, "How is a man able to be born when he is old? A man is not able to enter his mother's womb a second time to be born, is he?"

Jesus answered, "Amen, amen I say to you, unless someone is born of water and the Spirit, he is not able to enter the Kingdom of God. Whatever is born of flesh is flesh, and whatever is born of Spirit is spirit. Do not be amazed that I said to you, "You must be born again." The wind blows where it wills, and you hear its sound, but you do not know from where it comes or where it goes. So it is with everyone who is born of the Spirit."

Nicodemus answered and said to him, "How are these things possible?"

Jesus answered and said to him, "You are a teacher of Israel and you do not know these things? Amen, amen I say to you, that what we know, we speak, and what we have seen, we witness to, but you have not received our testimony. If I speak to you about earthly things and you do not believe, how will you believe if I speak about heavenly things? No one has ascended into heaven except the One who has descended from heaven, the Son of Man who was in heaven. As Moses lifted up the serpent in the desert, so must the Son of Man be lifted up, so that everyone who believes in him may not perish but may have eternal life. For God so loved the world that he gave his only-begotten Son so that everyone who believes in him may not be destroyed but may have eternal life."

Nicodemus is mentioned five times in Scripture, all in the Gospel of John. In addition to the above passage, John mentions that he is a Pharisee in the Sanhedrin and says that he brought a hundred pounds of spices for Jesus's burial. He came to Jesus at night—was it out of fear of what others might think? Yet, he made an act of faith that Jesus is truly a teacher from God as proven by the signs he performed. This indicates that Nicodemus did not merely see people healed, but he recognized that the miracles were signs pointing to the deeper reality that God had sent Jesus.

As is typical of Jesus, he responded by taking Nicodemus to a deeper level of faith, one by which he could make a commitment to enter the kingdom of God. This entrance requires a transformation so profound that it can only be described as a rebirth. As usual, Nicodemus responded on a human level by referring to the physical impossibility of re-entering his mother's womb. Jesus responded with a teaching on baptism, the rebirth by water and the Spirit. The Spirit, about whom Jesus will have much more to say at the Last Supper discourse, has a power and a will that cannot be controlled by human beings. So also this rebirth in baptism is beyond mere human controls and opens to a life led by the Holy Spirit.

Jesus told Nicodemus that there were more mysteries to learn than this. Jesus spoke of what he knows of the Spirit, the Father, and himself. He revealed that he came down from heaven and that he would be crucified, that is, lifted up on the cross like Moses's bronze serpent was lifted up in a tree, making the shape of a cross. While these mysteries about God and salvation may still have astounded Nicodemus, the important point underlying them all was knowing that God so loved the world that he sent his only begotten Son so that those who believe in him may have eternal life.

Let us pray.
Heavenly Father, you love us so much that you give us your own Son to die on a cross for us. For all of our sins and rejection of you, our lack of faith and our self-seeking, you give an infinite gift— your own beloved Son. You simply ask us to have faith in him in order to have eternal life. Yet, through him you also promise us your Holy Spirit, an infinite gift who leads and guides us to all truth and to you. By his power in the waters of baptism, give us entrance into your eternal kingdom. Draw us ever more deeply into your mysteries and fill us with the fullness of truth, so that through the eternity of heaven you will fill us with wonder and draw us ever closer to you and your infinite love. Amen.

Jesus Teaches the Disciples to Pray

Jesus and his disciples left Bethany, and he was hungry. When he saw a fig tree in the distance, which had leaves, he approached to find something on it. When he came to it, he found only leaves, for it was not the time for figs. Jesus responded by saying to the tree, "May no one eat fruit from you into eternity!" His disciples heard this, and they went into Jerusalem.

At dusk, they left the city. The next morning, when they were passing by, they saw the fig tree withered to the roots. Peter remembered and said to him, "Rabbi, see, the fig tree which you cursed has withered."

Responding, Jesus said to them,

Have faith in God. For amen I say to you, that whoever says to this mountain, "Get up and be thrown into the sea," and does not doubt but believes that what he says will happen, whatever he says will be his. Therefore I say to you, whatsoever you ask, having prayed, believe that you have received and it will be yours.

And if you remain praying, forgive, if you have anything against anyone, so that your Father who is in heaven may forgive you your trespasses. If you do not forgive, neither will your Father who is in heaven forgive your trespasses.

Once it happened when Jesus was praying in a certain place, as he rested, that one of his disciples said to him, "Lord, teach us to pray, as John also taught his disciples."

He said to them,

When you pray, say, Our Father, who are in heaven, holy is your Name. Your kingdom come, your will be done, on earth as it is in heaven. Give us this day our daily bread. And forgive us our trespasses as we forgive those who trespass against us. Lead us not into temptation but deliver us from evil.

The Gospels do not specify that it was this area or this cave where Jesus taught the Our Father, but in Crusader times people made a connection between these two passages in Mark and Luke and assigned this as the site.

At first, Jesus cursing the fig tree seems unfair since "it was not yet the season for figs." However, fig trees can produce an edible nub before the fruit is ready, and this tree did not have that. Second, some of the rabbinic speculation about the Messiah taught that when he came the grapes would be so large that each one would provide enough wine for a year. The fig trees would bear tremendous fruit and would bend down to give him fruit as he passed by. Given that background expectation, the fig tree was cursed because it did not offer its fruit when the Messiah needed it. In this way, the tree becomes a symbol of the

events of that day: After cursing the tree, Jesus found the money changers and sellers in the Temple and drove them out, and the "chief priests and scribes" became angry with him for doing this. After Jesus left the Temple, Peter saw the withered fig tree. When St. Mark divides an event such as this, he means for it to be interpreted using the material that is placed in between the two parts of the story. Here, the sellers, money changers, priests, and scribes are symbolized by the withered fig tree because they do not recognize Jesus either.

As is typical of Jesus, he did not dwell on the obvious—the success

of the curse—but took the disciples deeper to a teaching on the necessity of faith in God. He taught that faith is an act of total trust in God to answer one's prayers. Of course, one may have to wait to see the prayers answered, and it is not unusual for God to answer them in a way differently than we ask. That is why it is not such a good idea to overly instruct God how to answer a prayer; trust in him and let him answer as he will. The general experience of the saints is that even when the answer is different from original expectations, it is a better answer than the human plan.

Jesus added that forgiveness of others is a necessary prerequisite for receiving God's answers. This is consistent with the rest of Jesus's teaching, including the Our Father.

The Lord's Prayer always deserves contemplation of each part. It opens with a statement of faith: God is our Father who is in heaven. We start with the truth about God that he has revealed to us through Jesus his Son, and we want to remain committed to all the truths that he has revealed, trusting that his truth is far wiser than our speculations.

Our response to the act of faith is praise: Holy is your name.

Then we make a series of petitions that God's kingdom come and his will be done. Again, this petition is filled with faith that God's kingdom is more important than our human affairs, and his will is better for us and the rest of humanity than following our own will.

We ask for our daily bread, which is an act of faith to let the Father care for us daily. Jesus did not tell us to ask for a year's supply, or a month's or a week's supply. He wants us to trust in God each day.

Jesus wants us to ask the Father's forgiveness, but he sets a condition on it: We must forgive others. To that extent, we will be forgiven. It is a risk to pray like that, but it also summons us to become ever-more forgiving, even if we learn to do so in stages.

In the wilderness, Jesus knew what it was like to be led by the Holy Spirit into temptation, so he wants us to pray that we not be led into it. This does not imply that God ever tempts us. Rather, we should think about military generals, who want their troops to be safe. However, to win a war they must sometimes lead them out into battle against an enemy. They do so with the confidence that they will return victorious, but it is always a risk. Similarly, the Lord may lead us into temptations so we can defeat the evils around us, but Jesus certainly tells us to pray not to be so led. If we are led into temptation, then we pray that the Lord deliver us from the evil. We cannot depend on our own ability to defeat evil, but on his.

Dominus Flevit

The Lord Weeps Over the Destruction of the Temple

The small chapel of Dominus Flevit by Antonio Barlucci looks out from the Mount of Olives over the Old City of Jerusalem. While most of the churches in the Holy Land face the east, in accord with an ancient tradition, this church faces west, toward the city over which Jesus wept. Hence, the name of this chapel—Dominus Flevit—means "the Lord wept." Barlucci shaped the chapel in the form of a teardrop, and he kept the glass of the window facing west clear so that worshipers would be able to see the Holy City and be reminded of the whole world outside the Church, for whom Jesus wept, too.

CHAPTER ELEVEN

Next to the chapel are some mosaics and ruins of a fifth-century Byzantine church and fourteenth-century chapel built to commemorate the same events. In front of the chapel is a terrace with a wonderful view of the Old City of Jerusalem. One can see the Herodian stones at the southeast corner of the Temple and the whole Temple Mount, making it a good place for a group to consider Jesus's predictions of the fall of Jerusalem and its Temple.

The Temple was destroyed twice and desecrated various times. The Babylonians destroyed it after a two-year siege in July 587 B.C. The Greek king of Syria, Antiochus IV Epiphanes, desecrated it in 168 B.C. by setting up an idol of Zeus (with his face as the model for that of Zeus) in it. The Maccabean revolt recovered and rededicated it, as is celebrated on the Jewish holiday of Chanukah. In 63 B.C., Rome was asked to resolve a dispute between the high priest, John Hyrcanus, and his brother Aristobulus. Roman General Pompey attacked Jerusalem, captured Aristobulus, and killed twelve thousand Jews, including the priests at the altar, who were seeking refuge in the Temple. Then Pompey entered the Holy of Holies, which only the high priest was permitted to enter, and he laughed because it was empty (the Ark of the Covenant was long lost). Later he ordered the reconsecration of the Temple and placed John Hyrcanus II as the high priest and ethnarch of Judea.

After Herod the Great became king in 37 B.C., he began to rebuild the Temple into a magnificent complex around 20 B.C., and the project was completed in A.D. 64, sixty-seven years after Herod died. During the Jewish Revolt (A.D. 66–72), the Romans destroyed the Temple in August 70, thereby ending Israel's sacrifices and the authority of the priestly leaders, the Sadducees. For thirteen hundred years, until the present, the Al Aqsa Mosque at the location of the Temple remains the third-holiest Islamic shrine in the world (after Mecca and Medina).

Jesus consistently displayed a love of the Temple as his Father's house. He reacted angrily that money changers and sellers had turned "my house" into a den of thieves. Yet, when his disciples marveled at the beauty and magnificence of the Temple one evening in Holy Week, Jesus predicted the final destruction of the Temple forty years before it occurred. This is evident in the following passages.

Jerusalem, Jerusalem, who kills the prophets and stones those sent to her: how often I have desired to gather your children just as a hen gathers her chicks under her wings, but you would not. Your house will be left abandoned. For I say to you: you will not see me again until you say, "Blessed is he who comes in the name of the Lord!"

Jesus came out from the Temple, and his disciples approached to show him the buildings of the Temple. He answered them, "Do you not see all these things? Amen I say to you, not one stone here will be left upon another which is not thrown down."

When you see Jerusalem surrounded by armies, then know that her destruction is near. Then those who are in Judea will flee to the mountains and those in her midst will leave and those in the country will not enter her. For these days of her punishment are the fulfillment of all that is written. Woe to those who bear in the womb and those who are nursing in those days, for great will be the trouble on the earth and wrath to this people. They will fall by the mouth of the sword and will be taken captive to all the nations. Jerusalem will be trampled by the nations until the time of the nations is fulfilled.

Jesus's desire to gather Jerusalem to himself in loving protection was ongoing, but so was Jerusalem's refusal to come to him in faith.

Jesus's announcement that not a stone of the Temple would be left on a stone was fulfilled forty years later when Roman soldiers set the Temple on fire, despite the orders of General Titus to the contrary. The Western Wall (known by some as the Wailing Wall) still standing today is part of a retaining wall that surrounded the Temple Mount, but it was not part of the Temple itself, which today is replaced by the Al Aqsa Mosque.

Finally, Jesus warned that armies would surround Jerusalem and destroy her. The only safety would be in fleeing the city. In fact, when the Jewish Revolt began, the Christian community fled to Pella in Jordan. They remained there until after the complete destruction of the city, and then they returned to the area known today as Mount Zion. There they built a Christian settlement and a church on the site of the Upper Room.

Originally the name Zion applied to the ancient city, then to the Temple Mount, and finally to this Christian settlement. Because they had heeded Jesus's prophecy, the Christians not only survived the destruction, like chicks who had sought shelter with him, but they became the new Zion.

Flevit super illam ("He Wept Over It"), *by Enrique Simonet*

Why, O God, have you forsaken us forever?

Why does Your anger smoke against the sheep of Your pasture?

Remember your congregation, which you acquired long ago.

You redeemed the tribe of your inheritance,

Mount Zion, where you have dwelt.

Direct your steps to the eternal ruins

All the evil the enemy did in the sanctuary.

Your adversaries have roared within your meeting place.

They have set up their own banners as insignias.

It seemed like one bringing axes to a thicket of trees.

Now they shatter all the carved work with hatchet and hammers.

They set your sanctuary on fire,

They profaned the dwelling of Your Name to the ground.

They said in their hearts, "Let us maltreat them completely."

They burned all of God's meeting places in the land.

We do not see our insignia; There is no prophet anymore;

Not one of us knows how long this will last.

How long, O God, will the adversary taunt?

Will the enemy revile your Name forever?

Why do you withdraw your hand, your right hand?

From the midst of your bosom consume them.

Yet God is my King from the past;

He works salvation in the midst of the earth.

Let not the oppressed return in humiliation;

Let the afflicted and needy praise your Name.

Let us pray.

Lord, the Temple ruins remind us of the desolation that results from breaking your covenant and disobeying your law. Many people in the modern world, including many Christians, focus on themselves so much that your laws, righteousness, and holiness become irrelevant to their daily lives. The modern world has brought destruction and unrivaled mass murder by those who hate you, your truth, and your morals—nationalists, Fascists, Communists, racists, and abortionists. Therefore, we ask that you draw us close to you, like chicks, to find protection in you and your truth. By your grace keep us faithful to your new covenant and protect us from destruction in hell. Amen.

The view from the Church of Dominus Flevit, where Jesus wept over the city of Jerusalem

Gethsemane

Gethsemane is a hill that today includes some distinct properties through which a road leading to the top passes. At the top is the tomb of the Blessed Virgin Mary, next to which is a cave of the olive oil press. *Gath* is Hebrew for a press and *shemen* is the word for oil; hence, *Gethsemane* means the "oil press." This cave is where the eight apostles remained while Jesus, Peter, James, and John went a "stone's throw away" to pray. It is also considered the scene of Jesus's arrest.

Across the street is the Garden of Gethsemane, an enclosed grove of olive trees, and the Church of the Agony. Eight of the olive trees in this garden have root systems that date back twenty-five hundred years, meaning they may have been planted after the Jews returned from their

The Rock of Agony

that, no matter how bright the sun might be, it always seems like night inside the church. Inside the marble altar rail is a large outcropping of the natural stone, known as the Rock of Agony, where Christ prayed. Appropriately, the altar is immediately behind the Rock of Agony, to link the sacrifice of the Mass with Christ's passion and death. The base of the altar is stone in the shape of a cup, a reference to Christ's prayer that this cup of suffering pass from him. On the wall behind the altar are three large mosaics of Christ's agony, the betrayal by Judas, and the arrest of Jesus.

The Franciscan Friars prefer silence within the church itself, unless a group is celebrating Mass. At some rare times they allow groups to pray among the trees or in front of the church, or in the Gethsemane cave, if it is free.

exile in Babylon and they were already five hundred years old at the time of Christ. They still produce olives, and the Franciscans use the pits to make rosaries for special visitors, such as diplomats and Church leaders.

Next to this Garden is a church constructed on the foundations of the fourth-century church built here by St. Helena. The builders not only preserved the small patches of ancient mosaic floor under Plexiglas in the modern floor, but they imitated the very same mosaic patterns in the present church. The windows are made of a dark-purple alabaster so

Jesus's Agony and Arrest in Gethsemane

Then Jesus went with the disciples to an area called Gethsemane. He said to the disciples, "Sit here while I go over there to pray."

Taking Peter and the two sons of Zebedee, he began to be grieved and distressed. Then he said to them, "My soul is grieved to the point of death. Remain here and keep watch with me." He went a little further, fell on his face and prayed, "My Father, if it is possible, let this cup pass me by, but not as I will but as you will."

Then he came to the disciples and found them sleeping, so he said to Peter, "Are you not able to keep watch with me for even one hour? Keep watch and pray so that you may not enter into temptation: the spirit is willing but the flesh is weak."

A second time he went over to pray, saying, "My Father, if this cannot come to pass unless I drink from it, let your will be done."

Again he went and found them sleeping, for their eyes were heavy. He let them be and again going away, he prayed, saying the same thing a third time. Then he went to the disciples and said, "Are you sleeping still and resting? See, the hour is near and the Son of Man will be delivered to the hands of sinners. Get up, let us go; see, the one who betrays me is near."

He was still speaking when Judas, one of the twelve, came, and a large crowd with swords and clubs came with him from the high priests and elders of the people. His betrayer gave them a sign, saying, "The One whom I kiss is he. Seize him." He immediately approached Jesus and said, "Hail, Rabbi!" And he kissed him.

Jesus said to him, "Friend, why are you here?"

Then those who approached set their hands on Jesus and seized him. Then one of those who was with Jesus stretched out his hand, drew his sword, struck the servant of the high priest, and cut off his ear. Then Jesus said to him, "Return your sword to its place, for everyone who takes up the sword dies by the sword. Or do you think that I am not able to ask my Father and he would provide for me now more than twelve legions of angels? Then how would the Scriptures be fulfilled, since it is necessary?"

At that hour Jesus said to the crowd, "As if for a robber have you come out with swords and clubs to arrest me? Daily I sat in the Temple teaching, but you did not seize me. The whole of this has happened so that the writings of the prophets might be fulfilled."

Then all the disciples left him and fled.

Jesus and the eleven disciples left the Upper Room after the Last Supper and came to Gethsemane. Since spending the night inside was part of the requirement for proper celebration of Passover, the rabbis extended Jerusalem's city limits beyond its very crowded, walled city to include the Mount of Olives. Jesus, therefore, was keeping the Law completely by staying there. Also, Luke mentions that it was "his custom" to go to the Mount of Olives, which explains how Judas knew to lead the arresting party to him there.

After separating the usual three chosen disciples—Peter, James, and John—Jesus asked the three to "keep watch with me." One little-considered aspect of this scene is its connection with the High Priest's all-night vigil with the other priests before his celebration of Yom Kippur, the Day of Atonement. The younger priests

were to help him stay awake lest any inadvertent ritual impurity happen that would prevent him from offering the next day's sacrifices. However, here in Gethsemane, it is Christ, the High Priest according to the order of Melchizedek, who tries to keep his newly ordained priests of the new covenant awake as Jesus prepares to offer himself as the Lamb of God on the cross, the ultimate act of atonement for the whole human race for all eternity.

Archbishop Fulton J. Sheen loved to use this passage as his first request to his newly ordained priests: "Keep watch with me." He derived from this the importance of making a Holy Hour with Jesus, in which we spend time simply to be with him, share our hearts with him, and listen to him speak to our hearts. Frequently people are tempted to keep very busy with activity during a Holy Hour, perhaps because they do not know the proverb, "If the devil can't make you bad, he

will make you busy." Taking time with Jesus, especially in the presence of the Blessed Sacrament, is a way to extend the celebration of the Mass into a time of quiet attentiveness to Jesus Christ. It is a way for each Christian to take time in Gethsemane.

When I was growing up in Chicago, there was a custom to visit seven churches on Holy Thursday night. When I returned there to teach after graduate school, I began to practice this again. Then I invited some of the Jesuit scholastics (seminarians) to join me and see some of the old, ethnic churches that were especially decorated on that night. We do not have to wait until Holy Thursday for this; we can do this any day and every day that our churches are open, whether the Blessed Sacrament is exposed or reposed in the tabernacle. The key is to "keep watch" with Jesus and let him form our souls.

One last reflection comes in light of a prophecy from Isaiah, "On him was the chastisement that makes us whole, by his stripes we are healed." This prophecy refers not only to the stripes Jesus received in his scourging but to the whole process of his saving passion and death. His suffering heals those who turn to him in faith. Here in Gethsemane, Jesus was betrayed by one apostle with a kiss and abandoned by the other eleven. Through this he wins a grace to heal those many people who have been betrayed by a spouse's kiss or abandoned by a parent, child, spouse, or friend. Jesus meets each person who has been betrayed or abandoned within their experience because it is his as well. He has won an understanding that can comfort us. Let him meet us in our grief with the power of his saving grief so he can overwhelm our sadness with his faithful love.

Let us pray.
Lord Jesus Christ, you knew you had to suffer. The reason for which you came into this world was to become the ransom for our sin. Yet, your knowing the purpose of your pain did not take away your fear and repulsion of it. Knowing that your sheep would be scattered did not eliminate the agony of betrayal by a disciple and abandonment by the others. By this agony, heal us of our pains of betrayal and abandonment by our own loved ones. Give us the grace to join our sufferings with yours so as to bring good for the whole Church. Amen.

EAST OF JERUSALEM

Bethphage

A couple blocks east of the Ascension Chapel and the Church of Pater Noster is the Palm Sunday Church in Bethphage, a name meaning "house of unripe figs." This small Franciscan church was built in 1883 over the ruins of a Crusader church. In 1876 a rock was found by accident, which earlier pilgrims had identified as the meeting place of Jesus Christ with Martha and Mary. The Crusader paintings on the sides of this rock show an ass and her foal, a castle and some men, a group of people carrying palms, the raising of Lazarus, and a Latin inscription reading "Bethphage." Cesare Vagarini restored these in 1950 and later painted the frescoes on the church walls in 1955. An additional point of interest is behind the church, where Jewish-Christian tombs with rolling stones of the type that would have been used in Christ's tomb can be found.

CHAPTER THIRTEEN

The Procession Through the Streets of Jerusalem, *by James Jacques Tissot*

Christ's Triumphant Entry

On Palm Sunday, the Patriarch of Jerusalem and a large crowd of local Christians and pilgrims gather with palm and olive branches to walk from this church, through St. Stephen's Gate, to St. Ann church as a reenactment of Christ's entry into Jerusalem.

When they came near to Jerusalem, they came to Bethphage (House of Unripe Figs), at the Mount of Olives. Then Jesus sent two disciples and said to them,

Go to the village ahead of you, and you will immediately find a tethered ass and a colt with her. Loose them and lead them to me. And if anyone says something, say that the Lord has need of them, and immediately he will send them.

This whole thing happened so that the word of the prophet might be fulfilled, which says, "Say to daughter Zion,

'Behold, your king comes to you meek and mounted on an ass, a colt, the son of a beast of burden.'"

The disciples went and did as Jesus had commanded them. They brought the ass and the colt and laid their garments on them, and Jesus was seated upon them. Most of the crowd spread their garments on the road. Others cut branches from the trees and spread them in the road.

The crowds leading and those following cried out, "Hosanna to the Son of David! Blessed is he who comes in the Name of the Lord! Hosanna in the highest!"

When he entered Jerusalem, the whole city was stirred, saying, "Who is this?"

The crowds said, "This is Jesus, the Prophet from Nazareth of Galilee!"

Jesus would have rested the day before his entry into Jerusalem because it was the Sabbath; his entry into the city is one week before his glorious Resurrection. Immediately upon entering Jerusalem, he went to the Temple to clear out the money changers and sellers, and the next three days were spent teaching in its courts. Next came Christ's priestly actions: the Last Supper on Holy Thursday; his trials, sufferings, and death on Good Friday; a Sabbath rest in the tomb on Holy Saturday; and rising from the dead on Sunday.

The week of teaching in the Temple before his great self-sacrifice on the cross and his Resurrection is an interesting parallel with the week that the high priest of Israel spent in the Temple before the Day of Atonement offering of the sacrifices for his own sins and those of the nation. Though the high priest spent his time memorizing the ceremonies and studying Scripture, Jesus would spend his time in the Temple teaching words that would become part of the Gospels. Jesus was preparing to offer himself, the Lamb of God, as the sacrificial Lamb who would take away the sins of the world.

Jesus gave his disciples very specific instructions, something he would repeat when he told Peter and John to prepare the Last Supper. His instructions at Bethphage were clearly meant to effect the fulfillment of the prophecy in Zephaniah and particularly Zechariah, who described the messianic king coming to Jerusalem on a humble ass, with meekness. This is in contrast to Alexander the Great, who had ridden through the region to conquer Egypt and later Babylon and Persia while riding his magnificent war stallion, Bucephalos. Jesus consciously identified with the prophecy of the humble, meek Messiah.

Inside the Palm Sunday Church are murals depicting boys in trees, cutting down the olive and palm branches for the people to wave, even as the people do in the Palm Sunday procession to this day. These types of branches are used because of a local tradition that the olive and date palms are the most blessed of trees, since every part of them can be used. Their fruits are eaten; date pits are ground into flour for bread while olive pits burn hot for cooking; both have usable wood for building; and the olive leaves are used for smoking meats, while palm branches can become roofs of houses. These blessed olive and palm branches were used to bless Jesus as he entered Jerusalem.

The crowd acclaimed Jesus with quotations from Psalm 118, a passage which mentions people approaching the altar with branches. *Hosanna* in Hebrew means "save us." Jesus did not coordinate that aspect, but it fits with the fulfillment of prophecy that permeates this event.

Tombs at the Mount of Olives

Let us pray.
Lord Jesus Christ, you entered Jerusalem in triumph, only to be crucified and buried for our salvation. As we recall your triumphal entrance, may we be reminded to honor and worship you every day of our lives. By proclaiming you as Messiah and King, may we be open to the graces of salvation won for us at the cross and in the tomb. By our cries of "Hosanna in the highest," please save us. Amen.

Bethany

Bethany is now a small town just a couple miles from Jerusalem. Though today the town is mostly Muslim, two churches—one Greek Orthodox and the other Roman Catholic—commemorate Jesus's two visits to the home of Martha, Mary, and Lazarus. The Catholic Church of Martha, Mary, and Lazarus is built over the ruins of two Byzantine churches and a Crusader Benedictine convent. Small sections of the ancient mosaic floor are still visible inside the church and in the courtyard; sections of the medieval convent walls stand in the courtyard. The tomb of Lazarus is a few yards outside the church property and down a set of very steep stairs. Inside the church are four wonderful mosaics to commemorate Christ's visits to the town.

CHAPTER FOURTEEN

Jesus Visits Martha and Mary

Now it happened as they were going along that they came into a certain village. A certain woman by the name of Martha welcomed Jesus into her house. She also had a sister named Mary, and she sat at the feet of Jesus, listening to his word.

Martha was distracted with a lot of service. So she approached Jesus and said, "Lord, does it not concern you that my sister has left me alone to serve? Therefore tell her that she should assist me."

Jesus answered her, "Martha, Martha, you are concerned and troubled about many things. But one thing is necessary, and Mary has chosen the good part, which will not be taken away from her."

This episode occurs immediately after Jesus told the parable of the Good Samaritan in response to a lawyer's question about who is one's neighbor. That parable emphasized the importance of demonstrating care and service to those in need. However, here in Bethany Jesus de-emphasizes Martha's service in relation to Mary's willingness to listen to Jesus's word. This event and the story of the Good Samaritan place the importance of service and contemplation in tension. This juxtaposition shows the importance of both and discourages the Christian from neglecting either one.

Let us pray.
May we seek to serve our Lord and our brothers and sisters, yet may we also desire to be nourished by the word of Jesus, which strengthens our souls. May action and contemplation fill our lives in proportion to the call of Christ.

Prayer for Generosity
(St. Ignatius Loyola)
Dearest Lord, teach me to be generous. Teach me to serve you as you deserve; to give, and not to count the cost; to toil, and not to seek for rest; to labor and not to ask for any reward save that of knowing that I am doing your will. Amen.

Jesus Raises Lazarus from the Dead

A certain man was ill, Lazarus of Bethany, from the village of Mary and her sister Martha. Mary was the one who anointed the Lord with myrrh and dried His feet with her hair. Her brother, Lazarus, was the one who was sick. Therefore the sisters sent a message to Jesus, saying, "Lord, behold, the one whom you love is sick."

When he heard it, Jesus said, "This sickness is not to death but for the glory of God, so that the Son of God might be glorified through it." Jesus loved Martha and her sister and Lazarus. When, therefore, he heard that he was sick, he then remained in the place where he was for two days.

Then, after that, he said to his disciples, "Let us go to Judea again."

The disciples said to him, "Rabbi, just now the Judeans sought to stone you, and you are going there again?"

Jesus answered, "Are there not twelve hours in the day? If someone walks in the day, he does not stumble because he sees the light of this world. If someone walks around at night, he stumbles because he does not have the light in him." He said these things and after this he said, "Lazarus our friend is asleep, but I will go so that I might wake him."

His disciples said, "Lord, if he is asleep he will be saved." Jesus had been speaking about his death but they supposed that he was speaking about the sleep of slumber.

Then Jesus spoke to them openly, "Lazarus is dead. And I rejoice for your sake that I was not there, so that you may believe. But let us go to him."

Then Thomas, the one called the Twin, said to his fellow disciples, "Let us go, too, so that we might die with him."

Then, when Jesus came, he found that Lazarus had already been in the tomb for four days. Bethany was near Jerusalem, less than two miles away. Many of the Judeans had come to Martha and Mary to console them over their brother. Then, when Martha heard that Jesus had come, she went to meet him. Mary sat in the house.

Martha said to Jesus, "Lord, if you had been here, my brother would not have died. But even now I know that whatever you ask God, God will give you."

Jesus said to her, "Your brother will be resurrected."

Martha said to Him, "I know that He will be resurrected in the resurrection on the last day."

Jesus said to her, "I am the resurrection and the life. The one who believes in me, even if he die, will live. And everyone who lives and believes in me, will not die forever. Do you believe this?"

She said to Him, "Yes, Lord, I have believed that you are the Christ, the Son of God who has come into the world."

And having said these things she called

her sister Mary quietly saying, "The Teacher is here and is calling you." When she heard this, she got up quickly and went to him. Jesus had not yet come into the village but was in the place where Martha had met him. Therefore the Judeans, who were in the house with her to comfort her, saw her get up quickly and leave. They followed her saying, "She is going to the tomb so she may cry there."

Then, as Mary came to where Jesus was, she saw him, fell at His feet and said, "Lord, if you were here, my brother would not have died." Then Jesus saw her weeping, and the Judeans who had joined her were weeping; he was deeply moved in spirit and upset himself and said, "Where have you placed him?"

They said, "Lord, come and see." Then the Judeans said, "See how he loved him!" But some of them said, "Was not he who opened the eyes of the blind man able to do something so that this one would not die?"

Jesus again was deeply moved within himself, as he came to the tomb. It was a cave and a stone was set on it. Jesus said, "Take away the stone."

Martha, the sister of the dead man, said, "Lord, it will stink already, for it has been four days!"

Jesus said to her, "Did I not say to you that if you believed, you would see the glory of God?"

Therefore they took away the stone from where the dead man had been placed. Jesus lifted up his eyes and said, "Father, I thank you because you have heard me. And I know that you always hear me, but because of the crowd standing around I said this so that they may believe that you have sent me."

Then he cried out in a loud voice, "Lazarus, come forth!" Then the dead man came out, having been bound by the feet and hands with strips of cloth, and a face cloth was wrapped around his eyes. Jesus said to them, "Loose him and let him go."

Many of the Judeans who came to Mary and saw what Jesus had done believed in him.

The first section of this passage is concerned with the way Jesus brings his disciples to deeper levels of faith through the dialogue about Lazarus. Just as with the healing of the man born blind in John 9, so also is the healing of Lazarus directed to God's glory. The two-day delay until Lazarus's death was a component of manifesting God's glory, since the purpose was clearly to demonstrate that Jesus personifies life and resurrection, just as healing the blind man manifested that Jesus is the light of the world.

In the dialogue, the disciples were worried about the danger entailed in going to Judea, and they wanted to interpret Lazarus's "sleep" as a sign of physical recovery so none of them would have to travel to a dangerous place. However, Jesus's revelation of Lazarus's death is meant to call them to believe in him.

They had begun to believe in him at Cana when he performed his first sign of changing water into wine, and now Jesus wanted to work an even more powerful sign so as to deepen their faith more. Their only response was one of resignation to the inevitability of dying with him—something which they would actually avoid just a week or so later.

In the second section, Jesus arrived in Bethany, where his first encounter was with Martha. Her first statement seems to a be a bit of a reproof of Jesus for not having come immediately to heal the sick Lazarus, but she then expressed faith that Jesus could do something even though Lazarus was dead. Martha speaks for many people of faith who tell God how to operate his providence and plans, yet they maintain trust when God does not follow their suggestions.

Jesus responded by taking Martha (whose name means in Aramaic "Lord, come") to deeper levels of faith in the resurrection of the dead. She definitely believed in the resurrection at the end of time, but Jesus announced that he personifies resurrection and life and that belief in him is necessary to share in the resurrection to eternal life. She was so open to faith in him that she, like the woman at the well, came to believe that he is the Christ, the Messiah who is the Son of God come into the world.

Filled with this deepened faith, Martha called her sister Mary in the third part of this passage. Mary, too, reproved Jesus for not coming to Lazarus while he was still sick. This evoked grief and tears from Jesus, a manifestation of his true humanity immediately after Martha had professed his true divinity. This emotion moved him to take action.

In the fourth section Jesus approached the tomb and instructed the people to open it. True to the character Martha showed in Luke 10:40, she tried to worry Jesus about the bad odor. However, Jesus turned to praise the Father and speak to him that the crowd might come to have faith. At that point he did what only God can do: He raised the dead, and Lazarus came forth. Next he told the people to unbind Lazarus, so that they should do what they were capable of doing. This is the same pattern as at the multiplication of loaves and fish: He blessed, broke, and multiplied, while the disciples did what they were capable of, namely, distributing the

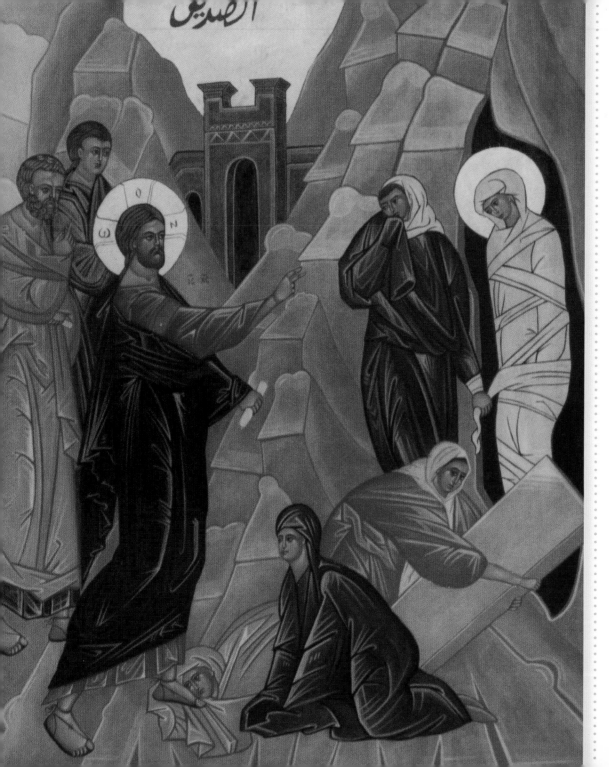

bread. So also in our lives, Jesus will do what only God can do, and then he will call us to do what we are able to do, requiring us to be ever attentive to the actions of grace and the calls to obey.

Let us pray.
Lord Jesus, even as Martha proclaimed you the Christ and the Son of God, you wept for your friend, Lazarus, like any human would. Your human affection overwhelmed you with grief, and you shared in the blessing you promised those who mourn. Yet, your divine love, which is the source of all blessing, raised Lazarus from the dead. Deepen our faith that you are the resurrection and the life, the Christ and Son of God, so that we may draw ever closer to you and grow in more wisdom from you. Amen.

Jericho

At the north end of modern Jericho stands a mound known as Tel es-Sultan. A tel is an artificial mound formed by the buildup of ancient civilizations. Tel es-Sultan is the site of ancient Jericho, the oldest city in the world. Its earliest ruins, including a stone watchtower, go back eleven thousand years to the Neolithic period.

In addition to being the site captured by the Israelites under Joshua, Jericho is neighbor to the Mount of Temptation. This traditional site of Jesus's temptations by the devil is but a short distance to the west. On the side of the mountain are small buildings, the cells of an ancient monastery that are still in use.

Jesus in the Wilderness

Then Jesus was taken into the desert by the Spirit to be tempted by the devil. And having fasted for forty days and forty nights, He was hungry at last. Then the Tempter came and said to Him, "If you are the Son of God, say that these stones will become bread."

He answered and said, "It is written, 'Not by bread alone will a man live, but by every word which comes forth from the mouth of God.'"

Then the devil took Him to the Holy City and stood Him on the parapet of the Temple and said to Him, "If you are the Son of God, throw yourself down, for it is written, 'He has commanded His angels about you, and they will bear you on their hands lest you strike your foot against a stone.'"

Jesus said to him, "Again it is written, 'You shall not tempt the Lord your God.'"

Again, the devil took Him to a very high mountain and showed Him all the kingdoms of the world and their glory. Then he said to Him, "These will I give You if You fall down and worship me."

Then Jesus said to him, "Be gone, Satan, for it is written, 'The Lord your God shall you worship, and Him alone will you worship.'"

Then the devil left Him, and angels came and served Him.

Temptation of Christ in the desert by the devil

The first point we notice is that the same Holy Spirit who hovered over Jesus at the Jordan River when he was baptized leads him into the desert to be tempted. We must be clear about the fact that the Holy Spirit does not tempt Jesus, since God tempts no one. However, the Holy Spirit does lead Jesus into the situation of fasting and prayer in which he becomes liable to Satan's temptations, much as an army is led out to battle in order to defeat an enemy.

A second point is that the temptations all come from Satan, not from within Jesus. He does not have the disordered desires within a human being due to the fall of Adam and Eve. Christ, like the first Adam, can be tempted only by forces outside himself. We see that here; we see it when the crowd want to make him their king after the multiplication of the loaves and fish; and we see it when

Peter rebukes him for predicting his suffering and death.

A third point is that Jesus refutes each of Satan's temptations with a quotation from Scripture, specifically from Deuteronomy: "Not by bread

alone will a man live, but by every word that comes forth from the mouth of God"; "You shall not tempt the Lord your God"; and "The Lord your God shall you worship, and him alone will you worship."

The eleven-thousand-year-old neolithic B-period stone tower was discovered at Jericho's oldest level of habitation

Interestingly, from the Mount of Temptation you can easily look across the Jordan Valley to the Jordanian side of the river, to the Plains of Moab. That is where Moses delivered the book of Deuteronomy to Israel. And here Jesus refutes Satan with Moses's words. The authority of God's Word and its wisdom are more powerful than the sophistry of Satan's temptations. From Jesus's example we can learn not to argue with temptation in terms of its own logic but to resist it with God's holy Word.

Fourth, in overcoming these temptations, Jesus wins for all humanity the grace to overcome temptation. We need not depend on our own acts of the will but can come to Jesus Christ and receive from him the grace to avoid sin and remain in virtue. St. Paul could thus say, "God is faithful, and he will not let you be tempted beyond your strength, but with the temptation will also provide the way of escape, that you may be able to endure it." Here at the Mount of Temptation we learn to always turn to Jesus Christ for the strength to reject evil and choose him.

Let us pray.
Lord Jesus Christ, in your fasting you won for us the grace to fast from the things of this world, so that we might be free from the materialism that can enslave us to the world. You overcame the temptations of the devil so as to free us from temptations that keep us in bondage. By the grace you won for us in overcoming temptation, make us free to serve you alone, with our whole hearts, minds, and souls. Amen.

Zacchaeus in the Sycamore Tree

South of Tel es-Sultan and close to the center of modern Jericho, a very old sycamore tree stands behind a fence in a small garden. The tree is now two thousand years old, and the New Testament city of Jericho is farther south.

Then Jesus entered and passed through Jericho. Behold, there was a man called Zacchaeus by name. He was the chief tax collector, and he was very rich. He wanted to see who Jesus was but was not able to do so on account of the crowd, for he was short in height. So he ran before and went up into a sycamore tree, so that he might see Him, for He was about to go through that place.

As He came to the place, Jesus looked up and said to him, "Zacchaeus, hurry down, for today it is necessary for Me to stay at your house." So he hurried down, and he showed himself to be joyful. When everyone saw him they murmured, saying that Jesus was going in to be a guest of a sinful man!

Standing firm, Zacchaeus said, "See, half of my belongings, Lord, I give to the poor. And if I have defrauded anyone, I will pay him back four times as much."

Jesus said, "Today salvation has come into this house, since he is a son of Abraham. For the Son of Man came to seek out and save the lost."

Jesus summoning Zacchaeus the publican to entertain him at his house, *by William Brassey Hole*

The great majority of Christians can relate to Zacchaeus: We rejoice that Jesus desires to be with us despite our sins. Most of us are grateful that the Son of Man "came to seek out and save the lost." However, some of us balk at the idea of making so thorough a restitution for past sins as does Zacchaeus—giving away half his goods and dividing up much of the other half to pay back those he has defrauded, which could have been a significant number. Nonetheless, we must note that Jesus announced the arrival of salvation to Zacchaeus's house only after he had decided to make restitution for his past sins.

People who work Twelve Step programs not only do a thorough moral inventory and confess their faults to another individual but also make lists of those they have offended so they can make amends (as long as the amends do not harm the other person). No one should be surprised that a Catholic priest, Fr. Edward Dowling, S.J., helped compose the Twelve Steps, drawing from his experience as a Christian and a priest. As challenging as the steps of Zacchaeus's conversion might be, we do well to meditate on them, learn them, and imitate them.

Let us pray.
Lord Jesus Christ, you became a welcome guest in the home of the sinner Zacchaeus. Your love evoked from him the works of righteousness and reconciliation. Lord, you also knock on the doors of our hearts, seeking to be a guest within.

Lord, we invite you into our hearts. Show us how to be reconciled with those against whom we have sinned. May your salvation come to our lives so that we may give you praise and glory. Amen.

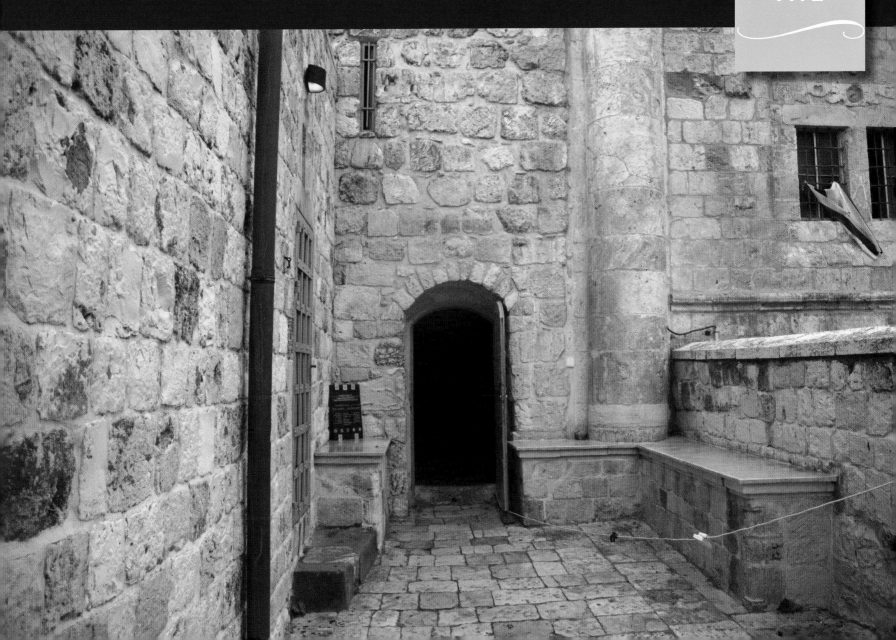

MOUNT ZION

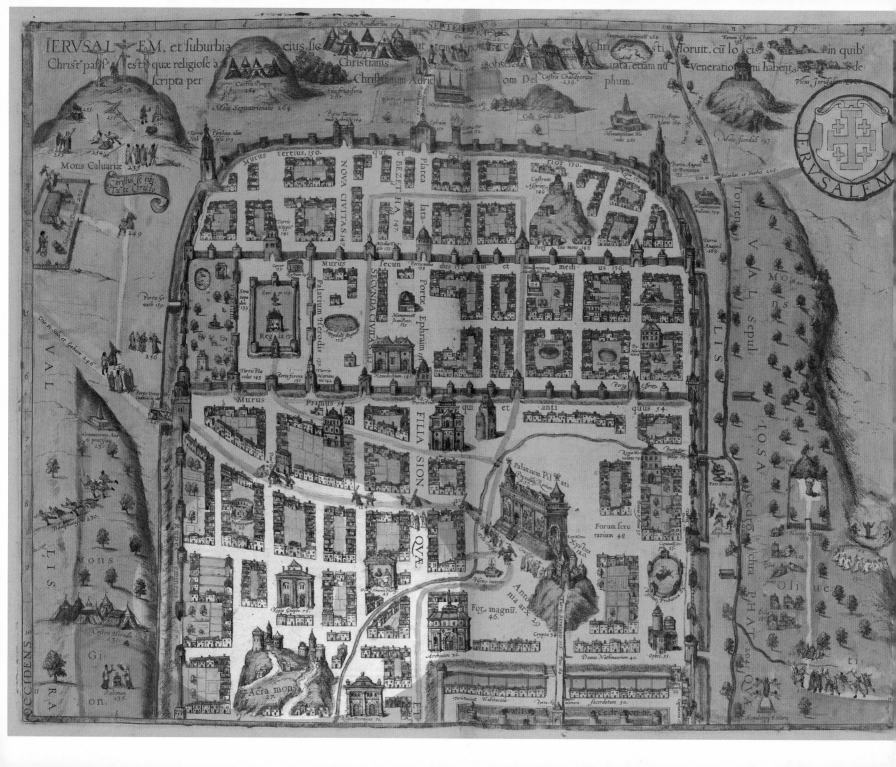

The Upper Room

The present Upper Room is a medieval building constructed over first-century foundations. On its first floor is a synagogue called the Tomb of David, where a niche, known as a *mihrab*, in the south wall indicates former use by Muslims. On the north side of the room is a *cenotaph*, that is, a memorial to King David's tomb. Behind the cenotaph is another niche, which follows the line of the first-century foundation.

CHAPTER SIXTEEN

If this building had been a synagogue, the niche behind the cenotaph would be directed toward the Temple, to show the connection between the worship in both buildings. However, this niche points directly toward Calvary and Jesus's tomb, indicating a Christian orientation.

An ancient mosaic map in St. George Church in Madaba, Jordan, portrays the first-century building, which was probably built by the early Christians who returned to Jerusalem in A.D. 72 or 73, after the Romans destroyed the city in A.D. 70. They chose this site because they remembered it as the location of the Upper Room. Christians worshiped in it until the Persians destroyed it in A.D. 614.

An outside staircase brings us to today's Upper Room. It is a Christian chapel built in the twelfth century and remodeled by the Franciscans in the fourteenth. Its use as a mosque began in the sixteenth century. It was restored to Christians with the establishment of the state of Israel in 1948.

Celebrating Mass is not permitted inside the Upper Room, so the Franciscans bought a bakery next door, to the north, and turned it into a very nice chapel, the *Coenaculum*. At the front is a life-size bronze depiction of the Last Supper. Jesus holds up a large round of bread that in fact is the tabernacle of the chapel. The Franciscans welcome pilgrims during regular visiting hours to pray before the Blessed Sacrament and to celebrate holy Mass.

The Upper Room is associated with a number of important biblical events, including the origins of four of the seven sacraments. Our prayer here will help us renew our faith in Christ's promise at the end of his public ministry to remain present with his Church throughout all time.

The Last Supper

The day of unleavened bread came, in which it was necessary to sacrifice the Passover. Jesus sent Peter and John, saying, "Go, prepare the Passover for us, so that we may eat."

They said to Him, "Where do You want us to prepare it?"

He said to them, "Behold, when you go into the city, a man carrying a water jar will meet you. Follow him to the house that he enters, and say to the master of the house, 'The Teacher says to you, Where is the guest room where I may eat the Passover with My disciples?' He will show you a large furnished upper room. Prepare it there."

When they went out, they found it just as He had said to them, and they prepared the Passover. When the hour arrived, He sat at table, and His apostles were with Him.

He said to them, "With longing I have longed to eat this Passover with you before My suffering. For I say to you that I will not eat it until it is fulfilled in the kingdom of God."

And having received the cup, He gave thanks, saying, "Take this and share it among yourselves. For I say to you that I will not drink from the produce of the vine until the kingdom of God comes." And taking bread, He gave thanks, broke it, and gave it to them, saying, "This is My Body, which will be given up for you. Do this in My memory." Likewise He took the cup after supper, saying, "This cup is the new covenant in My blood, which will be poured out for you.

"Nevertheless, see, the hand of the one who betrays Me is at table with Me. Certainly, the Son of Man is going according to what has been appointed, but woe to that man by whom Me is betrayed."

The Last Supper, *by Leonardo da Vinci*

They began to ask one another about who among them was about to do this thing. Then there was a dispute among them concerning which of them seemed to be greater.

He said to them, "The kings of the gentiles lord it over them, and those who have authority are called their benefactors. But not so for you. Let the one who is great among you be as the youngest, and the leader as one who serves. For who is greater: the one who is seated at table or the one who serves? Is it not the one who is seated at table? But I am in your midst as one who serves.

"You are the ones who have remained with me throughout my temptations. I am giving you a kingdom, as the Father has given to Me, so that you may eat and drink at My table in My kingdom. You will be seated on thrones, judging the twelve tribes of Israel."

Then the Lord said, "Simon, Simon, behold, Satan has sought you all, to sift you like wheat. But I have prayed for you that your faith may not fail. And when you have turned back, strengthen your brothers."

Peter said to Him, "Lord, I am ready to go with You both to prison and to death."

But Jesus said to him, "I say to you, Peter, the cock will not crow before you deny knowing Me three times."

While the Gospel of John has the longest Last Supper discourse by far, the Gospel of Luke contains a number of very interesting points to consider.

Jesus's instructions about finding the place for the Last Supper give us two of these points. Since women usually carried the daily water, the unusual sight of a man carrying a water jar would have been distinctive enough to observe. Such a man might not have a wife. In fact, the Upper Room is located in the old Essene Quarter of Jerusalem, where the core members of the Essene community were celibate.

Another point about Jesus's instructions is their lack of specifics. The directions did not give Judas enough information to pass on to the authorities, so the Last Supper would not be interrupted. Only later, in Gethsemane, would the authorities intercept Jesus.

Third, Luke's Gospel says that Jesus celebrated Passover on Holy Thursday. Yet the Gospels also mention that Good Friday was the Day of Preparation for the Passover. How can both be factual?

The Dead Sea Scrolls show that the Essenes used a solar calendar, according to which they celebrated the first day of Passover on a Wednesday, while the Sadducees and Pharisees followed a lunar calendar, by which the day of Passover would change every year. Interestingly, the Last

Supper is between both celebrations. Perhaps this indicates that it was a celebration of the Feast of Unleavened Bread. They did not have lamb; Jesus, "the Lamb of God," was the Passover Lamb at the meal.

Fourth, Jesus blesses the cup and gives it to the disciples, saying he will not drink of the fruit of the vine "until the kingdom of God comes." The Mishna mentions that someone serving at another person's Passover meal could not partake of the food but had to wait until he returned home to eat his own meal. Jesus's action indicates that he is acting as the servant. This further identifies Jesus as the Servant of the Lord of Isaiah 53, who will suffer for the forgiveness of us all, for our healing, and to make us righteous.

Fifth, the terminology and actions Jesus chooses at the institution of the Eucharist indicate that he means this to be understood as his real Body and Blood and as a sacrifice. He uses an emphatic form to state that the bread *is* his Body and the wine *is* his Blood of the new covenant. "Pour out" is the phrase used to describe what Moses did with the "blood of the covenant" from the animal sacrifices. The term *memory* referred to a type of sacrifice, and the word *do* was frequently used for offering sacrifices, especially non-animal sacrifices. Jesus intends to institute the Eucharist as a sacrifice that entails his continued presence, for his followers to take and eat.

Sixth, the command to "do" this in his memory institutes the second sacrament here, the priesthood. Since it is the nature of a priest to offer sacrifice, Jesus's command to the twelve to offer this memorial sacrifice constitutes them as his priests of the new covenant. They share in his priesthood, since Jesus is the one true high priest according to the order of Melchizedek.

Seventh, Jesus explains the apostles' roles as roles of service and not self-exalting searches for power. Yet he also promises to set them on thrones to judge the twelve tribes of Israel, indicating that their roles are very important. In particular, Peter will lead them and strengthen their faith, even after he falls. Peter denies that he will fall, but Jesus predicts that Peter will deny him three times. This will happen just down the street, at the house of Caiaphas (see chapter 18, on the Church of St. Peter in Gallicantu).

Finally, Jesus is fully aware of Judas's coming betrayal. This is not merely some accident of history; it was foretold in Scripture. Though the betrayal is within God's plan, still Judas is doomed to experience a "woe," the opposite of a beatitude. This is the consequence of his betrayal of the Son of Man.

Jesus Washes the Disciples' Feet

Before the Feast of Passover, Jesus knew that His hour had come when He would pass over from this world to the Father. Having loved His own who were in the world, He loved them to the end. When supper was being served, the devil had already put it into the heart of Judas Iscariot that he should betray Jesus.

Jesus knew that the Father had given everything into His hands and that He came forth from God and was going to God. He rose up from the table, put aside His outer garment, and taking a towel, wrapped it around Himself. Then He poured water into the basin and began to wash the feet of the disciples and dry them with the towel with which He was wrapped.

Then He came to Simon Peter, who said to Him, "Lord, do You wash my feet?"

Jesus answered and said, "What I am doing you do not know now, but you will know after these things."

But Peter said to Him, "You will not ever wash my feet!"

Jesus answered him, "If I do not wash you, you have no part with Me."

Simon Peter said to Him, "Lord, not my feet only, but also my hands and head!"

Jesus said to him, "One who is washed does not have need except for his feet to be washed, but rather the whole is clean. And you are clean, though not all." For He knew who was going to betray Him. Because of this He said, "Not all of you are clean."

When He had washed their feet, He took His garment and reclined at table again. He said to them, "Do you know what I have done for you? You call me Teacher and Lord, and you speak well, for I am. If therefore I have washed your feet, being Lord and Teacher, so you also ought to wash the feet of one another. For I have given you an example, so that just as I have done to you, you also should do. Amen, amen, I say to you: A servant is not greater than his lord, and an apostle is not greater than the one who sent him. If you know these things, blessed are you if you do them.

"Not about all of you do I speak. I know the ones I have chosen. But so that the Scripture might be fulfilled, 'The one who eats bread with Me has lifted up his heel against Me' [Psalm 41:9]. Now I speak to you before it happens, so that when it happens, you may believe that I AM.

"Amen, amen, I say to you: One who receives whomever I send receives Me. And whoever receives Me receives the One who sent Me."

The Gospel of John does not relate the institution of the Eucharist, though Jesus's explanation of the theology of the Eucharist is in John 6. The other Gospels do not relate the foot washing. Jesus's announcement in Luke that he will not drink of the fruit of the vine indicates that he is taking the role of a servant at the Last Supper; the foot washing in John's Gospel indicates the same thing. In both Gospels we hear Jesus explicitly say that he is a servant, even though he is their Lord. In both Gospels Jesus draws the conclusion that the disciples are to serve one another.

Here, too, the conversation with Peter is highlighted. Peter tries to be better than the rest by refusing to let Jesus wash his feet. However, when Jesus explains the action in terms of having a "part" with Jesus, Peter goes to the opposite extreme and wants his hands and head washed, too.

At this point Jesus introduces the fact that one of the twelve is going to betray him; that one is not "clean." During the Last Supper, Jesus will indicate to the beloved disciple the

Christ Washing the Feet of the Apostles, *by Meister des Hausbuches*

identity of the betrayer by giving Judas a piece of bread dipped in sauce, a gesture of friendship. At that moment Satan will enter Judas, and he will go out into the darkness. Later Jesus will refer to him as a "son of perdition."

Here Jesus explains that the betrayal was foretold in Psalm 41:9 and therefore is part of the plan of salvation. His goal is to bring the disciples to believe in him, to know that he is "I Am."

The Lord God revealed his sacred name to Moses in the book of Exodus. He instructed him to tell Israel that "I Am" sent him. When Jesus claims to be "I Am," he claims to be the Lord God, and he wants his disciples to believe this.

Jesus designates himself as "I Am" elsewhere: In John, when he walks on the water, he tells the disciples in the boat, "I Am," and later he says, "Before Abraham came to be, I Am."

When the soldiers say they are seeking Jesus, he answers, "I Am," causing them to fall backward.

Let us pray.
Jesus, as we consider the way you served your disciples by washing their feet, we cannot help but examine our lives in light of yours. We look at the humble tasks of washing our infants and children, and you give us a way to see our service to them in the light of your actions. When we wash and care for our sick or elderly relatives and friends, you are giving us a share in your kind and gentle ministry. At other times we might feel shame at avoiding serving some of the people around us.

Help us be like Mother Teresa of Calcutta and see you, Lord Jesus, in everyone around us, especially the poor and needy. May we share in your service to all and perform that service with you and for you, for the greater glory of God. Amen.

Thomas's Confession

The Upper Room was also the scene of our Lord's appearance to the disciples on Easter and the following Sunday:

When it was evening on that first day of the week, and the doors were closed where the disciples were for fear of the Jews, Jesus came and stood in their midst. He said to them, "Peace be with you!" As He said this, He showed them His hands and His side. Then the disciples who saw the Lord rejoiced.

Then Jesus said to them again, "Peace be with you! As the Father has sent Me, so I also send you." As He said this He breathed on them and said, "Receive the Holy Spirit: Whosesoever sins you forgive, they are forgiven them; whosesoever sins you retain, they are retained."

But Thomas, one of the twelve who was called the Twin, was not with them when Jesus came. The other disciples said to him, "We have seen the Lord!" But he said to them, "Unless I see in His hands the mark of the nails, and I put my finger into the mark of the nails, and I put my hand into His side, I will not believe."

After eight days His disciples were again inside, and Thomas was with them. Though the doors were closed, Jesus came and stood in the middle and said, "Peace be with you!" He said to Thomas, "Bring your finger here and see My hands, and bring your hand here and put it into My side. Do not be unbelieving but believing."

Thomas answered and said, "My Lord and my God!"

Jesus said to him, "Because you have seen Me, Thomas, you have believed. Blessed are they who do not see but believe."

As with Mary Magdalene at the tomb and the disciples in Emmaus, this is a story of conversion to belief in Jesus's Resurrection. The ten disciples who saw him on Easter Sunday night rejoiced when they saw the wounds in his hands and side, though Luke adds that they first thought Jesus was a ghost. Jesus had to prove he was physically alive by letting them touch him and by eating with them.

At that point Jesus reiterated his gift of peace, breathed on them, and told them to receive the Holy Spirit. Jesus thus gave them the power to forgive or retain sins, something that would be possible only if they heard people's confessions and made a judgment about their repentance. This was the institution of the third sacrament of the Upper Room—confession, or reconciliation. Emphasis on the telling of sins brings out the fact that it is confession; emphasis on God's

merciful forgiveness brings out the reconciliation side of it.

The absent Thomas does not believe the testimony of the other ten disciples. Famously, he must touch Jesus. Though Jesus is not in the room when Thomas makes his demand for proof, Jesus is fully aware of it. On this following Sunday he insists that Thomas touch the wounds.

The disciples in the Upper Room witness those wounds—glorified, visible, and touchable after the Resurrection. These healing wounds of Jesus are eternally available for healing.

Let us pray.

Lord Jesus, may we come to believe in you ever more fully. May our faith in all you have done—in your miracles, healings, saving death, and glorious Resurrection—and in your full humanity and divinity ever fill us with joy.

Continue to speak your peace to our hearts, so that we may overcome any fears we have of the world. Make us bold proclaimers of you and your gospel truth to our world. Make us instruments who let sinners know they can find reconciliation and forgiveness of sins by the power of your death and Resurrection. Make us comforters of the sick and the emotionally wounded, so they can receive the power of your wounds to heal all of theirs.

Breathe on us, and send us forth by the power of your Holy Spirit. Without him we can do nothing; by his power we can fulfill the Father's will and serve you. May our service be solely for your greater glory. Amen.

Pentecost

When the Day of Pentecost was being fulfilled, everyone was gathered together in the same place. Suddenly there was a sound like a strong wind, and it filled the whole house where they were sitting. Divided tongues were seen by them, like fire, and they rested upon each one of them. Everyone was filled with the Holy Spirit, and they began to speak in other tongues, as the Spirit gave them speech.

Staying in Jerusalem were pious Jewish men from all the nations under heaven. When this sound happened, the crowd came together and were amazed, because each one heard them speaking in his own language. All were amazed and astounded, each one saying to the other,

"Are not all of these who are speaking Galileans? How do we each hear in our own language in which we were born—Parthians, Medes, Elamites, and those who dwell in Mesopotamia, Judea, Cappadocia, Pontus and Asia, Phrygia, Pamphylia, Egypt, and the area of Libya that is near Cyrene, and the Roman visitors, both Jews and converts, Cretans and Arabs! We hear them speaking of the great things of God in our own tongues."

All were surprised and perplexed, saying to one another, "What does this mean?" Others mocked, "They are full of sweet wine!"

Peter, standing with the eleven, raised his voice and declared boldly to them, "Jewish men and all who dwell in Jerusalem, let this be known to you, and pay attention to my words. For not as you suppose are these men drunk, since it is only nine o'clock. Rather, this is what is said through the prophet Joel,

"'And it will be in the last days, says God, I will pour out My Spirit on all flesh, and your sons and your daughters will prophesy. Your youth will see visions, and your elders will dream dreams. In those days I will pour out My Spirit on My men servants and maidservants, and they shall prophesy. I will put wonders in the heavens above and signs on the earth below. And everyone who calls on the Name of the Lord will be saved.'

"Israelite men, hear these words: Jesus the Nazorean was a man appointed by God for us in power, wonders, and signs, which God did through Him in our midst, as you yourselves know. This One, delivered up through the hands of the lawless, by the definite plan and foreknowledge of God, you killed, crucifying Him. God has raised Him, loosing the pangs of death, because it was not possible for Him to be held by it.

"For David says about Him, 'I saw the Lord before me through everything, for He is at my right hand, so that I will not be moved. Therefore my heart rejoices and my tongue is glad, since even my flesh dwells in hope. For You did not let my soul remain in Hades, neither did You let my bones see corruption. You

have made known to me the ways of life and given me fullness of joy in Your presence.'

The listeners were stung to the heart, and they said to Peter and the rest of the apostles, "What must we do, brothers?"

Peter said to them, "Repent and be baptized, each one of you, in the name of Jesus Christ for the forgiveness of sins, and you will receive the gift of the Holy Spirit. Because the promise is for you and your children, and for all who are far away, who call upon the Lord our God."…

They who gladly accepted his word were baptized. On that day were added about three thousand souls.

The disciples—including the Blessed Mother and the apostles, adding up to 120—were gathered for the Jewish Feast of Pentecost, also called the Feast of Weeks and the Harvest Festival. This feast celebrates the wheat harvest and the giving of the Law to Israel through Moses on Mount Sinai. Israel was commanded to gather together in Jerusalem. For that reason many pilgrims were in the city.

Instead of the Law written on tablets of stone, the Lord sends the Holy Spirit to be a law within hearts and a source of empowerment. That Christ would baptize those who believe in him with the Holy Spirit and power has been foretold by both John the Baptist and Jesus. Now the Holy Spirit comes upon the assembled followers of Christ like a mighty wind, and individual flames of fire alight upon each of them, so that both the whole community of the Church as well as each individual receives the gift of the Holy Spirit. They speak in tongues, and the foreign pilgrims from Asia, Africa, and Europe hear them and understand them in their own multiple languages.

This becomes the opportunity for Peter to demonstrate his leadership and speak the first sermon of the Church. The promise of the coming of the Holy Spirit of God exists in the Old Testament, but it was not a prominent part of Jewish theology. Therefore Peter begins by saying that the disciples are not drunk, as some suppose, but are filled with the Spirit promised in Joel as a sign of the final days.

Next Peter links the promised gift of the Holy Spirit with Jesus of Nazareth, who proved his power by miracles, especially his Resurrection. This, too, was predicted by David, who stated in Psalm 16:8–11 that his body would not see corruption. Peter clarifies that this prediction could not apply to David, whose body lies corrupted in his tomb. Therefore it applies to his descendant, the Messiah Jesus, who rose from the dead.

This "stings" the crowd "to the heart," and they ask for instructions on how to respond to this revelation. Peter calls them to repent and be baptized, which they proceed to do, and three thousand new believers from around the ancient world are added to the Church. They will bring their new faith home and prepare for the coming of the apostles and disciples as missionaries, to establish the Church throughout the known world.

Modern Christians can compare their situation with that of the apostles and disciples on that Pentecost, when the whole of the Church was about 120 members and the world either knew nothing of Christ or was hostile to him. The Lord took the disciples on an amazing adventure and accomplished much through them. He invites the Church today to continue to proclaim the truth about Jesus. Like the first Christians, we must depend on the power of the Holy Spirit poured out on Pentecost, the beginning of the fourth sacrament of the Upper Room, confirmation.

The Holy Spirit seals our souls with an eternal character to empower us to build up the Church by the exercise of his various gifts. Let us step out into the world as the apostles stepped out of the Upper Room, and proclaim the Gospel in fidelity to the truth of Christ and in power.

Let us pray.

Lord, without you we can do nothing; with you we can accomplish all you command us to do. Fill us with your Holy Spirit, and send us forth into the world as your missionaries. Equip us to speak well and clearly of you, to announce the Gospel boldly and humbly, and to love the people to whom you send us as you yourself love them.

Come, Holy Spirit, fill the hearts of your faithful, and kindle in them the fire of your love.

Send forth your Spirit, and they shall be created, and you shall renew the face of the earth.

O God, who did teach the hearts of your faithful people by sending them the light of your Holy Spirit, grant us by the same Spirit to have a right judgment in all things and evermore to rejoice in his holy comfort. Through Christ our Lord, Amen.

Church of the Dormition of the Blessed Virgin Mary

The Dormition Abbey is a German Benedictine monastery begun in 1898 and finished in 1911. It is built over the traditional site of the Blessed Virgin Mary's Jerusalem home, near the Upper Room.

The Byzantines first built the Church of the Pillar here, including a pillar from Caiaphas's house. In A.D. 415 they enlarged this church and renamed it *Hagia Sophia* (Holy Wisdom). Like all other churches of the area, it was destroyed in the Persian invasion of 614. Some of its ruins are visible on the level below the gift shop and cafeteria of the present abbey.

The large upper church is dominated by an enormous mosaic of the Blessed Mother holding Jesus in her arms, her right hand pointing to him. Above them are mosaics of prophets who predicted Christ's birth of a virgin in Bethlehem—including Isaiah, Jeremiah, and Micah—to show the connection between the Old and New Testaments.

We descend some stairs to a lower chapel, at the first-century street level. In the center is a most distinctive statue of the Blessed Mother laid out in death on a bier, which is covered by a mosaic depicting an embroidered cloth. Above this statue is a small dome with mosaics of figures looking down on the statue. In the center is Jesus Christ, and around him are women of the Bible who prefigure Mary—Eve, the mother of the human race; Miriam, who sang God's praises; Jael, Esther, and Judith, who saved Israel from her enemies; and Ruth, the ancestor of David and of Jesus. We read about Mary's passing in this chapel.

The Death of Mary

The New Testament does not describe the death and Assumption of the Blessed Virgin, but some of the Fathers tell the story based on ancient tradition. Page 132 contains a selection from *The Book of the Passing of the Most Holy Virgin, the Mother of God*, which is attributed to second-century St. Melito of Sardis but was actually written later. Like all of the earliest forms of the tradition, it claims that Mary's Assumption happened in Jerusalem.

One day, two years after Christ overcame death and ascended into heaven, Mary wept as she prayed at home. An angel greeted her, "Hail, O blessed of the Lord, who saved Jacob by His prophets. I have brought you a palm branch from the Lord's paradise. Instruct someone to carry it before your bier after you are taken from this body."

Mary said, "I ask that all the apostles of the Lord Jesus Christ be gathered together so I might see them again."

The angel responded, "By the power of my Lord Jesus Christ, all the apostles shall come to you."

The angel then departed in a great light. Mary put on her best clothes and went to the Mount of Olives to pray:

"I would not have been worthy to receive You, Lord, if You had not had mercy on me. Nevertheless, I guarded the treasure which You committed to me, so I pray that no power of hell may harm me. You, Lord, are God blessed for ever, world without end."

Then Mary returned home. Soon the apostles, summoned by the Lord, arrived at her home. They greeted her, saying, "Blessed are you by the Lord who made heaven and earth!"

Mary said, "Peace be to you, my most beloved brothers! God did not deprive me of your presence! See, I am going the way of all the earth, and the Lord has brought you here to comfort me. Let us keep watch until I depart from the body."

For three days they praised God. Then they saw the Lord Jesus come with a multitude of angels and a great light. The Lord said to His mother, "Come, you most precious pearl, enter into the treasury of eternal life!"

Mary fell on her face, worshiping God, and said, "Blessed be Your glorious Name, O Lord my God! You have kept Your promise to me, your Handmaid. You know, O King of Glory, that I have loved you with my whole heart. Receive me, your maidservant."

Then Mary got up, laid herself on her bed, gave thanks to God, and gave up her spirit. The apostles saw her soul, which was whiter than all snow or metal or silver glistening with light.

Then Jesus said to St. Peter, "Take the body of Mary and bear it to the east side of the city, where you will find a new tomb. Place it there and wait until I come to you."

Three virgins prepared Mary's body for burial. It shone so brightly that they could not look at it. The body of the blessed Mary was like a lily, with the sweetest fragrance issuing from it. St. John led the funeral procession, carrying the palm which the angel had brought to Mary, while the other apostles carried her bier, singing, "Israel has come out of Egypt! Alleluia!"

The Tomb of the Blessed Virgin Mary

Across the street from the Garden of Gethsemane, low on the Mount of Olives, is a cave containing Our Lady's tomb. This was a Jewish Christian church from the earliest centuries, and Byzantine churches were built here in 455 and in the late sixth century. The Persians destroyed the church in 614, but it was rebuilt by 680. During the Crusades it became a Benedictine convent church. It is now the property of the Armenian Orthodox Church, with Greek and Ethiopian chapels.

The present entrance and much of the interior structure date from Crusader times. The tomb of Queen Melisande of Jerusalem was built in 1161 inside the entrance, at the seventh of the forty-seven steps that descend to an edicule containing Our Lady's tomb. The Franciscans celebrate Vespers (Evening Prayer) at Our Lady's tomb on the Feast of the Assumption. When no liturgies are being celebrated, the priests very kindly welcome pilgrims to come to the tomb and pray.

The following continues the story from *The Book of the Passing of the Most Holy Virgin, the Mother of God*, by St. Melito of Sardis. It describes Mary's burial and Assumption.

The apostles carried Mary to the Valley of Jehoshaphat, where the Lord showed them a new tomb. They placed her body there, shut the tomb, and waited outside its door, as the Lord had told them. Then suddenly, the Lord Jesus Christ appeared with a multitude of angels and said, "Peace be with you!"

They answered, "Let Your mercy be upon us, Lord, since we place our hope in You!"

Jesus said, "Before I ascended to My Father, I promised you who have followed me that you would sit on twelve thrones, judging the twelve tribes of Israel. Now, I dwelt in this Woman whom I chose from the tribes of Israel, according to My Father's command. What do you want me to do with her?"

Peter answered, "Lord, you chose Your Handmaid to become Your immaculate chamber before all time.

It appears right to us, Your servants, that since You overcame death and now reign in glory, likewise should You raise Your Mother and take her with You, rejoicing in heaven."

The Savior said, "Be it done according to your will!"

The Lord commanded St. Michael the Archangel to bring the soul of the holy Mary. Then St. Michael rolled away the stone of the tomb. The Lord said, "Rise up, My Love and my Kinswoman: You did not suffer corruption by union of the flesh, and neither shall you suffer dissolution of the body in the tomb!"

Immediately Mary rose up from the grave and blessed the Lord and worshiped Him. "I am not able to give you worthy thanks, O Lord, for the innumerable benefits which You have promised to me, Your Handmaid. Let Your name be blessed forever, O Redeemer of the world, you who are

the God of Israel."

Then the Lord kissed her and departed. He delivered her to the angels, who led her to Paradise.

A number of other stories about Our Lady's Assumption exist, but a common theme is the assembly of the apostles before Mary's death. This attributes the Assumption to an early period, when they were still alive. (St. James, the son of Zebedee, was the first apostle to be martyred, in A.D. 42.)

While the Church has never stated definitively whether the Blessed Mother died or was assumed without passing through death, the dominant teaching of the Eastern Fathers is that she died before her Assumption. By the fourth century they celebrated the feast of her Dormition, or "falling asleep" in death. St. Epiphanius of Salamis (A.D. 310–403) wrote about Mary's death and Assumption in his *Panarion* (*The Refutation of All Heresies*). St. Jacob of Sarug (A.D. 451–521), nicknamed the "Flute of the Holy Spirit," taught that she died before the Assumption, as did St. Gregory of Tours (died 594), St. Modestus of Jerusalem, and many other Fathers. They point out that Mary died in imitation of Jesus, who was without original sin.

Notice, in the second part of the *Passing of the Most Holy Virgin,* that when Jesus seeks the opinion of the twelve, on the basis of the authority he has given them to judge the twelve tribes of Israel, Peter is the spokesman, as he is throughout the Gospels and Acts.

Mary's Assumption reminds all Christians of God's ultimate destiny for each person. We are not to be pure spirits in heaven for all eternity; rather the bodies of all people are to be raised gloriously from the dead. In the Old Testament we read that Enoch (Genesis 5:24) and Elijah (2 Kings 2:11) were taken up to heaven, prefigurements of Mary's Assumption.

In Revelation 12 the woman who gives birth to the Messiah is clothed with the sun and crowned with stars and has the moon under her feet. This is the scene of the Blessed Mother's glory that St. Epiphanius referred to in discussing the Assumption, and it is the First Reading at Mass on that feast day. Because of her Assumption into glory, we address Mary as "our hope" in the *Salve Regina*.

One last reflection is connected with a line in the *Passing of the Most Holy Virgin*: Jesus says, "Rise up, My Love and My Kinswoman." This points to his joy in raising his mother and in reuniting with her in heaven. I remind people who have lost loved ones, especially parents who have lost children, that just as Mary received ecstatic joy in being with Jesus again, so will they be filled with joy in their reunion with their loved ones.

Keeping watch at the foot of the cross

We do well to remember that we, like Mary, need to live in faith and holy virtue so that we may be worthy to join our Lord Jesus, Blessed Mary, the saints, and all our loved ones in heaven. Keep that reunion of love in mind as you continue your earthly pilgrimage to the ultimate destination, the heavenly Jerusalem.

Why Jerusalem instead of Ephesus?
Many Christians believe that the Assumption took place in Ephesus, thinking that Mary accompanied St. John there. Certainly Jesus, as he was dying on the cross, entrusted his mother to the beloved disciple. St. John eventually went to Ephesus, and the traditional site of his tomb is there.

However, we know that St. Paul was the first apostle to go to Ephesus, in A.D. 53, and he stayed until A.D. 55. He left St. Timothy as the bishop of Ephesus and later wrote two epistles to him. Neither Acts nor the epistles to Timothy mention John. It does not seem that he arrived in Ephesus until about A.D. 70.

By then Mary would have been about ninety. It is possible she lived to this age but the various traditions about her Assumption mention the presence of the apostles, most of whom had been martyred by A.D. 70.

The presence of the first-century tomb, the very early Jewish Christian church, plus successive Byzantine and Crusader churches, in addition to the testimonies of St. Melito and the majority of early Fathers, add weight to the belief that the Assumption took place in Jerusalem.

Let us pray.
Hail, Holy Queen, Mother of mercy, our life, our sweetness, and our hope:
To thee do we cry, poor banished children of Eve;
To thee do we lift up our sighs, mourning and weeping in this valley of tears.
Turn then, most gracious Advocate, thine eyes of mercy toward us,
And after this our exile, show unto us the blessed fruit of thy womb, Jesus.
O clement, O loving, O sweet Virgin Mary.
Pray for us, O Holy Mother of God, that we may be made worthy of the promises of Christ.

Church of St. Peter in Gallicantu

In gratitude for French assistance in the Crimean War, the Turkish sultan gave the ruins of the house of the high priest Caiaphas to the French Congregation of the Assumptionists. They built a church (1928–1932) over the excavation, with a chapel on each of its levels. This is a good place to consider our Lord's trial before the high priest Caiaphas and the Sanhedrin.

Outside the church is an ancient street, which once led from Mount Zion to the gate near the Pool of Siloam. Through that gate Jesus Christ and his disciples would have left the city to go to the Garden of Gethsemane. Remains of a sixth-century monastery church have also been found on this spot.

The Trial of Jesus Before Caiaphas

Those who had seized Jesus led Him to Caiaphas the high priest, where the scribes and elders were gathered. Peter followed Him from a distance, up to the court of the high priest. Then he entered inside and sat with the servants, to see the end. The high priests and the elders and the whole Sanhedrin sought false witnesses against Jesus so that they might put Him to death, but they did not find any. Many false witnesses came forward, but they did not find anything.

Finally, two false witnesses came forward and said, "This man said, 'I am able to destroy the temple of God, and after three days I will rebuild it.'"

The high priest rose up and said to Him, "Do you answer nothing? What are they testifying against You?" But Jesus was silent. The high priest said to Him, "I adjure You by the living God that You say

to us whether You are the Christ, the Son of God."

Jesus said to him, "You have said it. Furthermore I say to you, from now you will see the Son of Man seated at the right hand of the power and coming on the clouds of heaven."

Then the high priest tore his garments and said, "He has blasphemed! What further need have we of witnesses? See, now you have heard His blasphemy! How does it seem to you?"

They answered, "He deserves death!" Then they spit in His face and beat Him. Some slapped Him, saying, "Prophesy to us, Christ! Who is it who is hitting You?"

The entrance of the Church of St. Peter leads to a large chapel decorated with many mosaics related to the Last Supper, Jesus's trial, Peter's denial, and the crucifixion of Jesus. For instance, the south wall depicts the young John leaning on Christ's breast to learn the identity of the betrayer. A panel below that shows the elderly John on Patmos writing the opening line of his Gospel: "In the beginning was the Word."

One niche with a tabernacle shows Mary Magdalene with Holy Land penitent saints Mary of Alexandria and Peligie. The niche on the opposite side of the main altar shows the Good Thief, St. Dismas, with two Holy Land penitent men, Saints Dositheus and William.

The back (west) wall depicts the Blessed Virgin seated, with the nails, crown of thorns, and lance head resting on her womb. Simeon's prophecy, "A sword shall pierce your heart" is quoted here.

The north wall has a mosaic of Jesus looking directly at Peter after the three denials, while a panel below shows Peter as pope, holding the keys of authority and wearing a triple tiara, with the quote: "You are Peter, and on this rock I will build My Church, and the gates of Hades shall not prevail against it. I will entrust to you the keys of the kingdom of heaven."

These mosaics call us to see that the events of Christ's suffering and death changed not only the lives of the immediate witnesses but also lives down through history. Each person who considers these events in faith can allow them to transform his or her life. A whole new destiny is in store for those who receive the forgiveness of sins as did Peter, Mary Magdalene, and Dismas. Meanwhile those who do not come to Christ in faith—even many influential people—become unknown once they die. Or perhaps they are remembered for their misdeeds, as are Judas, Caiaphas, and Pontius Pilate.

The most striking mosaic is the very large depiction of the trial scene on the wall behind the main altar. Jesus stands in the center, bound to two soldiers. The members of the Sanhedrin have their arms raised, voting for his death, while Caiaphas tears his garments. Above Jesus two angels are lowering a cross, the inevitable result of the trial. Above them God the Father holds a hand over his eyes, to avoid looking at the

injustice of his Son's condemnation.

The injustice involves the false witnesses and the traps to get Jesus to testify against himself. When Caiaphas asks Jesus to state the truth about himself—namely, that he is the Christ, Son of God—he is condemned. Note that Caiaphas's question uses the exact words Peter said about Jesus: "You are the Christ, the son of the living God." At that time Jesus recognized that the Father had given Peter this statement of faith. Now these very words become a cause of slapping and mockery and condemnation to death.

Peter's Three Denials

This site takes its name from the Latin word *Gallicantu*, meaning "cock's crow." This is in commemoration of Peter's three denials of Jesus "before the cock crows thrice." A golden rooster sits on the roof of the sanctuary.

Peter was sitting outside in the courtyard when a maidservant approached him, saying, "And were you not with Jesus the Galilean?"

He denied it before everyone, saying, "I do not know what you are talking about."

He went out into the gateway, but another maid said to those who were there, "This one was also with Jesus the Nazorean!"

Again he denied it with an oath, "I do not know the Man."

After a little while those standing by approached Peter and said, "Truly you

Non novi illum.
Lc 22, 57

also were with them, for your accent makes it clear."

Then he began to curse and swear, "I do not know the Man!" And immediately a cock crowed. Then Peter remembered the word which Jesus had said to him, "Before the cock crows you will deny Me three times." So he went outside and wept bitterly.

The chapel just below the main floor of the Church of St. Peter leads us to meditate on this scene from Matthew's Gospel. Three icons stand at the front. In the first Peter has just denied Jesus a third time, saying, "I do not know him," as Jesus looks him in the eye. We see a fire in the background of this icon, and Peter does not bear a halo.

The second icon portrays St. Peter in a cave, weeping in grief over his failure to stand up for Jesus. Already, in this act of repentance, he has his halo. His repentance is the first step toward sanctity.

In the third icon a fishing boat is in the background as Jesus and Peter stand next to another fire, on which there are loaves and fish. This depicts Jesus's threefold question, "Do you love me?" and Peter's threefold affirmation of love.

Another good place to pray these verses is on the porch outside the church. There a bronze statue set portrays the maidservant, a soldier, and Peter around a fire next to a pillar, upon which a rooster sits.

Though Peter was the very one who professed, through the Father's inspiration, that Jesus is the Christ, the Son of God, now he denies even knowing Jesus. Ironically, his earlier words, "You are the Christ, the son of the living God," become the high priest's in condemning Jesus: "I adjure You by the living God that You say to us whether You are the Christ, the Son of God."

Peter had enough courage to enter the high priest's courtyard to see what would happen, but here he clearly acts out of fear. Many Christians throughout the ages have related with Peter, because they have done the same—not only when standing up for the faith entails persecution but even when it brings mere mockery or ostracism. Sometimes we lack the courage to turn away from temptations that face us.

We each can learn from Peter's repentance, particularly in contrast to Judas's despair and suicide, that salvation is available to each sinner. Jesus's gaze into our hearts when we sin is not one of rejection but a summons to true contrition and reconciliation. This is what Peter experienced when he professed his love of Christ three times and Christ affirmed his role as the shepherd of the Church.

Jesus's Prison

The most important level of the Church of St. Peter is the lowest one, which served as a prison in Caiaphas's time. Shelves are carved into the limestone walls of the cells, with something like handles carved above them. Here prisoners would sit or lie down, their hands tied with ropes or chains to the handles.

From these cells one walks down to an ancient water cistern that was used as a high-security cell. Prisoners were lowered by ropes through a hole at the top. One picture portrays Jesus being lowered into this pit after his trial before Caiaphas, to await his transport to Pilate's court in the morning.

Jesus was betrayed to the officials by his own disciple, abandoned by the majority of his disciples, denied by the leader of the twelve, and placed in total darkness at the bottom of this pit. Such aloneness was part of

the suffering by which Jesus heals those who believe in him, as Isaiah prophesied: "Upon him was the chastisement that made us whole, and by his stripes we are healed." All who experience such aloneness and abandonment may want to consider this dungeon and pray the following psalm with Jesus.

O Lord, the God of my salvation,

by day I called out, by night my cry is
    before You!

Let my prayer come before You.

Turn Your ear to my cry!

For my soul is sated with troubles,

and my life has come near to the world of
    the dead.

I am counted with those who go down to
    the pit;

I have become like a man who has no
    strength.

Among the dead am I free,

like the slain who lie in a grave,

whom You remember no longer

and who are cut off from Your hand.

You have placed me in the deepest pit,

in dark places, in the depths.

Your wrath rests upon me.

With all Your waves You overwhelm me....

Your wrath has passed over me;

Your terrors have silenced me....

You have distanced friend and neighbor
    from me;

my only friend is darkness.

Let us pray.

*Lord Jesus, you entered the depths of
suffering, going ever more deeply into
human pain. You experienced the
darkness of abandonment and loneliness.
We often experience this due to our own
fault, but you did nothing to deserve it.
Draw us ever closer to you when we are
in such darkness, so that we may know
that you are truly our companion; we are
not alone.*

*Your abandonment effected the
redemption of the world. Let us join our
sufferings and difficulties to yours for the
good of your Church.*

Jesus, I trust in you.

NORTH OF JERUSALEM

Emmaus

The location of Emmaus is not certain. Most ancient manuscripts say Emmaus was 60 stadia from Jerusalem (a stadion was 607 feet), while others say the distance was 160 stadia. Archaeologists have not conclusively identified any site as the New Testament Emmaus, though there is evidence for its existence in written sources.

Three sites claim to be Emmaus. One is 160 stadia (about nineteen miles) west of Jerusalem, near Latroun, where the ruins of a Byzantine church commemorate Jesus's meal with his two disciples. Another is in Abu Ghosh, about 60 stadia (seven miles) west of Jerusalem. A third site—my favorite—is north of Jerusalem, where a Franciscan church sits alongside a section of ancient Roman road.

CHAPTER NINETEEN

Jesus Meets Two Disciples on the Road

On the same day that the tomb of Jesus was found to be empty, two disciples went to a village by the name of Emmaus, sixty stadia distant from Jerusalem. They were talking with each other about everything that had happened. As they were talking and arguing, Jesus Himself came near, going along with them. Their eyes were held back from recognizing Him.

He said to them, "What are these words which you are discussing with each other as you walk?"

They stood, sad. One, by the name of Cleopas, answered Him, "Are You the only inhabitant of Jerusalem who does not know the things which happened in her these days?"

"What things?" He said.

"The things about Jesus of Nazareth! He was a prophet powerful in word and deed before God and all the people.

And how the high priests and our leaders handed Him over to a death sentence and crucified Him! We were hoping that He was the one about to redeem Israel. But along with all these things, this is the third day since all these things happened. Moreover, some of our women shocked us: They were at the tomb at dawn, but they did not find His body! They said they even saw a vision of angels who said He is alive! And some from our group went to the tomb, and they found it so, just as the women had said. But Him they did not see."

He said to them, "O senseless and slow in heart to believe in all the things that the prophets have said! Were not these things necessary, that the Christ should suffer and come into His glory?" And beginning with Moses and through all the prophets, He interpreted for them all the Scriptures about Himself.

As in the meeting between Mary Magdalene and Jesus outside the empty tomb, the disciples on the road to Emmaus do not easily recognize him. A key to this is that they did not expect to see him raised from the dead, even though he foretold the resurrection. The holy women went to the tomb to anoint Jesus's corpse, not wait for him to rise again. The two disciples heard that the tomb was empty and that angels told the women Jesus was raised from the dead, but they left that evidence hanging in the air, not committing themselves to an interpretation of it.

Jesus's first response to the two disciples is to upbraid them for not understanding the prophecies of the Messiah's suffering, death, and resurrection. He then expounds on the meaning of each prophecy in Scripture, which here could only refer to the Old Testament.

Jesus explains that the Old Testament predicted his suffering, death, and resurrection. The disciples apparently held the more typical view that the Messiah would "redeem Israel" along a political model. That is why the death seemed like such a disaster and why the resurrection did not compute for them. By demonstrating that the suffering, death, and resurrection were part of God's prophesied plan and not a mere fluke that sat on a precipice of failure, Jesus gave a new meaning to the preceding events.

In fact, Jesus led the disciples to understand that the death and resurrection meant much more than the success of Jesus; they were the conquest of sin and death, as the Old Testament hinted. Jesus's understanding of prediction and fulfillment is so important that, when he appears to the disciples in the Upper Room that night, he explains the same Scriptures again to this larger group.

While it is natural to wonder why St. Luke did not lay out Jesus's list of citations at this point, we can glean them from the other Gospels and the book of Acts. Various sermons there quote the Old Testament texts that are being fulfilled in the people's midst. The New Testament cites the Old Testament 360 times, so we too can learn to recognize this extremely important link between prophecy and fulfillment.

The Meal at Emmaus

They came near to the village to which they were going, and He gave the impression that He was going further. They urged Him saying, "Stay with us because it is evening and the day is already coming to an end." So He went in to stay with them.

As He reclined at table with them, He took bread, blessed and broke it, and gave it to them. Their eyes were opened, and they recognized Him, but He disappeared from them.

They said to each other, "Was not our heart burning within us on the road, as He opened the Scriptures for us?" They departed in that same hour and returned to Jerusalem. They found the eleven and some others gathered together, who said, "Truly the Lord is risen! He has appeared to Simon!" Then they related what had happened on the road and how He was made known to them in the breaking of the bread.

The disciples recognized Jesus in the breaking of the bread

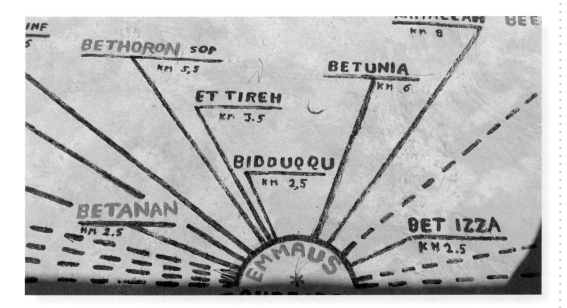

After acceding to the disciples' request to stay with them, Jesus performs the same sequence of actions as at the multiplication of loaves and fish and at the Last Supper (which these two disciples did not attend): He takes bread, blesses it, breaks it, and gives it to them. This experience evokes their recognition of him, at which point he disappears. This is when they also recognize the burning that was in their hearts as he "opened" the Scriptures to them on the road. They experience a conversion to faith in his Resurrection, as Mary Magdalene did once she recognized him.

We do well to consider the conversion of these disciples to faith in Jesus's Resurrection. They—like Mary Magdalene, Peter, Thomas, the other apostles, the crowd in Matthew 28, and Paul—have to undergo this conversion. Once they accept the Resurrection, they run back to Jerusalem to tell the other disciples. These disciples will go out into the whole world, so convinced of the risen Lord Jesus that they are willing to die rather than deny him. This is a thoroughgoing conversion upon which the Church still rests. St. Paul described Jesus's death and Resurrection as a matter "of first importance."

In the Emmaus incident we can see that a Liturgy of the Word before the Liturgy of the Eucharist evidences a link between the two "tables" at Mass: We are fed by the Word and by the Body and Blood of Christ. We never isolate them but see their integrity in the life of the Church until this day.

Let us pray.

Lord, you are the Word made flesh. You speak to us in every word of Sacred Scripture. Fill us with the same Holy Spirit whom you sent to inspire the prophets and apostles, so that our hearts might burn with the Good News of your revelation. Let the same Holy Spirit direct our prayer, especially at Holy Mass, so that we might recognize you in every Eucharist and keep our attention on you, for you are Lord forever and ever. Amen.

Jacob's Well

The edge of the West Bank town of Nablus is the site of Jacob's Well. We enter the Greek Orthodox property where a church is under construction, and below this structure is a chapel with a well in the center. The Greek priest permits visitors to lower the bucket with a rope from a hand crank, at which point the great depth of the well becomes evident.

No other well fits the description of the well mentioned in John. So this is the place where we consider the Lord's meeting with the Samaritan woman.

CHAPTER TWENTY

Jesus Meets the Samaritan Woman

Since Jesus knew that the Pharisees had heard that He was making more disciples and baptizing more than John—although Jesus Himself did not baptize but only His disciples did—He left Judea and went to Galilee again. It was necessary for Him to pass through Samaria. Therefore He came to a city of Samaria called Sychar, neighboring the area that Jacob gave to his son Joseph. There was the well of Jacob.

Jesus was weary from the journey, so He sat down at the well. It was the sixth hour (twelve noon). A Samaritan woman came to draw water.

Jesus said to her, "Give Me to drink." For His disciples had gone into the city so that they might buy some food.

Then the Samaritan woman said to Jesus, "How is it that You, a Jew, ask from me, a Samaritan woman?" (For Jews do not associate with Samaritans.)

Jesus answered her, "If you knew the gift of God and Who it is saying to you, 'Give Me to drink,' you would ask Him and He would give you living water."

The woman said to Him, "Lord, You do not have a bucket, and the well is deep. Therefore, where do You have living water? You are not greater than our father Jacob, who gave us the well, who drank from it, as did his sons and cattle?"

Jesus answered her, "Everyone who drinks from this water will thirst again. Whoever drinks from the water that I will give to him will not thirst forever. Rather, the water that I will give him will become in him a spring of water leaping up to eternal life."

The woman said to Him, "Lord, give me this water, so that I will neither thirst nor come back here to draw water!"

He said to her, "Go, call your husband and come here."

The woman said to Him, "I do not have a husband."

Jesus said to her, "You have spoken well, 'I do not have a husband,' for you have had five husbands, and the one you have now is not your husband. What you have said is true."

The woman said to Him, "Lord, I see that You are a prophet. Our fathers worshiped on this mountain, and You say that Jerusalem is the place where it is necessary to worship."

Jesus said to her, "Believe Me, woman, the hour is coming when neither on this mountain nor in Jerusalem will you worship the Father. You worship what you do not know; we worship what we know, for salvation is from the Jews. But an hour is coming and is now here when true worshipers will worship the Father in spirit and in truth. For the Father seeks such worshipers. God is Spirit, and it is necessary that those who worship Him worship Him in spirit and truth."

The woman said to Him, "I know that the Messiah, who is called Christ, is coming. When He comes, He will announce everything to us."

Jesus said to her, "I am, the one speaking to you."

At this His disciples came. They were amazed that He was speaking with a woman; however, no one said, "What are You looking for?" or "Why are You speaking with a woman?" Then the woman left her bucket and went back to the city and said to the men, "Come, see a man who told me everything I ever did! Is He not the Christ?" They came from the city and went to Him.

Jesus asks a Samaritan woman of Sychar for water from Jacob's Well, *from the Codex of Predis*

Many scholars point out that John's Gospel contains the strongest statements of Christ's divinity, particularly the times he says, "I Am," in a way that identifies him with God's self-identity in Exodus:

God said to Moses, "I Am who I Am." And He said, "Thus will you say to the children of Israel, 'I Am sent me to you.'"

Jesus clearly states, "Before Abraham came to be, I Am." Many other "I Am" statements make this connection to God, and the Jewish people knew Jesus was saying that he is equal to God. "The Father and I are one." These statements sometimes overshadow St. John's equally clear descriptions of Christ's human nature: "The Word became flesh"; Jesus's grief for Lazarus; and here, in his weariness and thirst.

Many commentators also point out that this Samaritan woman came to draw water at noon, rather than the usual times, at sunrise and sunset. Perhaps she was ostracized in the village because her present husband was not her own, and so she wanted to avoid the times when the other women congregated to draw water and talk. Whatever the reason, her coming at this hour leads to a providential meeting with Jesus. Note how Jesus begins this, like so many dialogues in John, with a statement on a physical, everyday level and then takes it to deeper levels. From his request for water to slake his thirst, he moves to offering the woman a water that will satisfy her thirst. While she responds on the physical level of buckets and a deep well, he piques her interest in a water

for everlasting life. When she asks him for that water, he asks for her husband.

At this point she gives a misleading statement: "I have no husband." Notice that Jesus does not accuse her of lying or of being a hussy; rather he agrees with her: "You have spoken well, 'I do not have a husband,' for you have had five husbands, and the one you have now is not your husband. What you have said is true." In saying this he again speaks a deeper truth than she is willing to speak.

The woman realizes that Jesus is not merely some man ordering her to give him water, nor is he an idle braggart; he is "a prophet." This realization that he knows her past life leads her to change the subject to theological differences between the temple of the Jews in Jerusalem and that of the Samaritans on Mount Gerizim. (This latter temple still exists today, overlooking the site of Jacob's Well.) Jesus cuts through this theological diversion with two points: (1) Salvation is from the Jews; and (2) in the future "true worshipers will worship the Father in spirit and in truth," since "God is Spirit."

The woman responds with an act of faith that the Messiah is coming, and then Jesus takes her to the next level by asserting, "I am the one who is speaking with you." This overly literal translation indicates that this is another of Jesus's "I Am" statements, which at the very least hints at his divinity. This highlights the movement from his very human exhaustion and thirst to an acknowledgment of his Messiahship and divinity.

Jesus's Food

Meanwhile, the disciples asked Him, "Rabbi, eat!"

He said to them, "I have food to eat which you do not know."

Therefore the disciples said to one another, "Has someone brought Him something to eat?"

Jesus said to them, "My food is that I do the will of the One who sent Me and that I complete His work. Do you not say, 'It is the fourth month and the harvest is coming'? Behold, I say to you, raise your eyes and see the fields that are white for harvest. Already the reaper receives his reward and gathers fruit for eternal life, so that the one who sows rejoices and so does the one who reaps. For in this is the word true: 'One is the sower and another is the reaper.' I have sent you to reap that for which you did not labor. Others have labored, but you have entered into their labor."

Many of the Samaritans from that city believed in Him through the witness that the woman gave, "He told me everything I ever did." Therefore, as the Samaritans came to Him, they asked Him to stay with them, so He remained with them for two days. Many more came to believe in Him through His word. They said to the woman, "We no longer believe because of what you said. We ourselves have heard, and we know that He is truly the Savior of the world."

The drama of the scene includes the arrival and wonderment of the apostles and the woman's haste to tell everyone in the village of this encounter with one who might be the Messiah. The apostles want to give Jesus food; he already has the food of doing the Father's will as nourishment. The Samaritans invite him to stay, and come to faith in him.

This episode is a model of the conversion process. As we hear Jesus speak, and as we let him take us to deeper and deeper levels of meaning, we have to make a decision about his role as Messiah and his divinity, as well as the humanity we meet on the surface. Acceptance of him in faith, self-knowledge, and repentance will transform our lives and bring us into the great adventure of bringing still others to know him as Savior and Lord.

Let us pray.
Lord, you know us better than we want to know ourselves. Despite your full awareness of our sinfulness, you desire to give us the Holy Spirit. You want him to spring up within us with the waters of eternal life and joy. Make us open to your forgiveness and to the gift of the Holy Spirit, so that we might always worship you in spirit and in truth. Amen.

WESTERN GALILEE

Nazareth

Basilica of the Annunciation

The building that dominates the center of Nazareth is the Basilica of the Annunciation. We enter a courtyard that contains mosaics of the Virgin Mary and the Christ Child from around the world. They wear clothing in the styles of various parts of Europe, Africa, and Asia.

Then we come to the bronze front doors and the front wall, which depicts the life of Christ in metal and stone. We enter a wide floor space that leads to a depression in the building. Here the history of worship is revealed at this sacred place.

In 1730 the Franciscans obtained permission to build a church at the ruins of a Crusader church; some pillars of that early church remain. The wall to the north is from the Crusader church. Looking into the lower level, you can see the stone outline of a fifth-century Byzantine church; just outside those walls are mosaic floors and a baptistery from a third-century church.

At the center of attention on the lower level is a small grotto in which an altar stands. Inscribed are the Latin words "Here the Word was made flesh." The turning point of salvation began here, when the Blessed Virgin Mary accepted the angel Gabriel's invitation to become the Mother of God the Son, and the Holy Spirit overshadowed her so that the Word might take flesh within her womb.

A new basilica was begun in 1955 and dedicated in 1969. This required the demolition of the 1730 church

and allowed for the excavation of the various archaeological levels of the site. During these excavations a fragment of first-century pottery (an *ostracon*) was found containing the verse Isaiah 7:14 in Aramaic. To better understand the mystery of the Incarnation, let us look at that passage: "Behold, a virgin shall conceive and bear a son, and she will call his name 'Immanuel.'"

The first-century ostracon links the grotto with the earliest Christians of Nazareth. Thus the churches at the different levels of civilization until the present connect us with that faith. In this faith we bend our knees at the words "The Word became flesh," particularly when we pray the Angelus or profess the Nicene Creed on the Feast of the Annunciation. We are humbled by the fact that God the Son would empty himself of the glory of heaven to be conceived in the womb of the Virgin Mary in Nazareth.

The Annunciation to the Blessed Virgin Mary

In the sixth month [after John the Baptist's conception], the Angel Gabriel was sent from God to a city of Galilee, by the name of Nazareth, to a Virgin betrothed to a man named Joseph, of the house of David. The name of the Virgin was Mary. When he came to her he said,

"Hail, Graced One! The Lord is with you!"

She was disturbed at his word, and she wondered what sort of greeting this might be.

The angel said to her, "Fear not, Mary: you have found favor with God. Behold, you will conceive in your womb and bear a Son, and you will call His name Jesus. He will be great, and He will be called the Son of the Most High, and God will give Him the throne of David, His father. He will rule over the house of Jacob forever, and His kingdom will not come to an end."

Mary said to the angel, "How will this be, since I do not know man?"

The angel said to her, "The Holy Spirit will come upon you, and the power of the Most High will overshadow you. Therefore, the One who is to be born will be called holy, the Son of God. And behold, Elizabeth your kinswoman has conceived a son in her old age. This is the sixth month for her who was called sterile, for nothing is impossible with God!"

Mary said, "Behold the handmaid of the Lord; let it be according to your word." And the angel left her.

This scene contains Christological and Marian components. First, the Christological aspect comes with Gabriel's description of the son whom Mary is to call Jesus. Seven descriptions of Jesus are given, each of which emphasizes his exalted qualities: He will be great, he will be called Son of the Most High, he will have the throne of his father David, he will rule over the house of Jacob, his kingdom will never end, he will be called holy, and he will be called Son of God.

Three of these qualities reveal his divinity: being called the Son of the Most High, Son of God, and holy. The other four indicate a humanity by which Jesus fulfills Old Testament prophecies about the Davidic kingship—most poignantly in Ezekiel:

I will shepherd my sheep, and I will make them lie down....

I will establish over them one shepherd, and he shall shepherd them, David, My servant. He will shepherd them, and he will be a shepherd for them.

These verses describe how the Lord and the Davidic king will shepherd the people; Gabriel's message shows that Christ fulfills both sides of that prophetic promise. Also, these descriptions of Christ provide another type of background to "The Word [who is God] became flesh and dwelt among us." Truly he is God; truly he is man, a man who fulfills prophecies.

The Marian aspect of this scene is very rich, too. Gabriel greets Mary as "the one who has been graced" and tells her that the Lord is with her and she has found favor with God. One clear emphasis in these words is that the Virgin Mary had received tremendous grace from God prior to Gabriel's mission. This grace and the presence of the Lord within her have opened her mind and will to do whatever he might ask of her.

The gracious state of Mary's soul does not grant her every intellectual illumination. Thus she asks, "How shall this be, since I do not know man?" Note that while Zechariah asked Gabriel, "How will I know this?" Mary asks, "How shall this be?" He wanted proof; she wants instructions.

Finally, Mary's response is a model for all Christians: "Behold the handmaid of the Lord; let it be according to your word." She accepts her lowly status before God and willingly agrees to "let it be" according to God's word. At that moment she does not physically feel the presence of the Son of God in her womb, but she believes it and acts upon that faith.

This scene provides one of the sources for the Hail Mary. Let us slowly pray this prayer, focusing on the words of Gabriel: "Hail Mary, full of grace, the Lord is with thee."

St. Joseph Church

Outside the upper church of the basilica and across the courtyard is the Church of St. Joseph. While crossing the courtyard, you can see the excavation of a number of ancient homes, caves in which entrances and holes for smoke were cut. This was the Holy Family's neighborhood.

A hundred and ten yards across the courtyard, we enter St. Joseph Church, which contains stained-glass windows and paintings depicting the life of the Holy Family. Stairs lead to a crypt chapel, with a Jewish Christian baptistery. Gratings in the floor allow you to look down into a cave known as St. Joseph's workshop. The annunciation of the birth of Jesus to St. Joseph can be remembered here.

The birth of Jesus Christ was like this: When his mother, Mary, was betrothed to Joseph, but before they came together, she was found to be with child by the Holy Spirit.

Joseph her husband, being a righteous man and not wanting to make a spectacle of her, decided to divorce her in secret. As he was thinking about these things, behold, an angel of the Lord appeared to him in a dream, saying,

"Joseph, son of David, do not fear to take Mary as your wife, for what is begotten in her is from the Holy Spirit. She will bear a Son, and you will call His name Jesus, for He will save His people from their sins."

All of this happened so that the word from the Lord through the prophet Isaiah might be fulfilled,

"Behold, a virgin will conceive and bear a Son, and she will call His name Immanuel," which means "God is with us."

Joseph woke up from sleep, and he did just as the angel of the Lord commanded him, and he accepted his wife. He did not know her until she bore a son, and he called His name Jesus.

Joseph's experience of the Incarnation has parallels to the Blessed Virgin Mary's experience. Both are well aware of the natural course of conceiving children: Mary asks Gabriel how she could conceive without knowing man; Joseph assumes that Mary did conceive with another man.

Joseph did not act with indignation to shame Mary but decided on a secret divorce. Like Mary, who pondered mysteries in her heart, so Joseph thought about the events and his options. This thoughtful, reflective quality in the face of unknown and unclear realities easily flows from righteousness, a component of wisdom.

As careful as his thoughts might be, Joseph cannot come to an understanding of the true facts of the situation without the aid of revelation. The angel in his dream reveals that the child is begotten of the Holy Spirit, not of another man. The child is a boy, whom Joseph will name Jesus, the same name given to Mary by the angel in Luke. Here the angel adds that the name, which means "salvation," indicates that the child will save his people from their sins. This revelation confirms Isaiah's oracle that a virgin shall conceive and bear a son, thereby connecting this event with Old Testament prophecy.

At this point righteous Joseph proves himself to be a man of faith: He believes both the angel's word and the prophecy, and he does everything he is commanded to do. For the most part his life of obedience will entail the fulfillment of many ordinary details of life: He will take care of the duties of feeding and housing the Holy Family, and he will teach Jesus the skills of carpentry.

Joseph will die in obscurity. His death is not recorded in the Gospels, but the lack of any mention of his name during Christ's public ministry indicates that he passed away before that point. Despite that obscurity, Joseph continues to be a strong and much loved intercessor in the Church. Thousands of churches are named for him, and nearly every Catholic church has an altar dedicated to St. Joseph.

Jesus in the Temple

Another event to recall in Nazareth is the finding of the child Jesus in the Temple and his return with his parents to their home:

He went down with them and went to Nazareth, and He was subject to them. His mother pondered these words in her heart. Jesus advanced in wisdom, age, and grace before God and men.

We can consider a number of elements of this episode in the Nazareth context. First, it indicates that the Holy Family lived out the Law of Moses, which required Israel to assemble in Jerusalem three times a year for the great feasts—Passover, Pentecost, and Tabernacles. St. Luke mentions that it was the family's custom "every year" to join hundreds of thousands of fellow Jews in the festival of Passover.

The reason to mention this particular occasion is the unusual occurrence of Jesus's staying behind in Jerusalem. Mary and Joseph are worried about him; Jesus is calmly in his Father's house. This indicates Jesus's awareness of his identity as God's Son.

We also see here his parents' lack of understanding of what Jesus is about. Their holiness did not always give them clarity about Jesus's words and deeds; these remained a mystery to be pondered.

We can learn from the silent years of Nazareth about our own need to contemplate the mysteries of the Faith. Perhaps it will be many years before we come to a proper perspective on how and why God acts the way he does with us. However, we can see that the Blessed Mother meditated and pondered. Most likely she acquired further insight into Jesus's life and mission after the Resurrection and Pentecost.

Jesus himself continued to grow in wisdom, age, and grace during the quiet years in Nazareth. Various cult and esoteric writers have tried to claim that Jesus spent the next eighteen years in Egypt, India, Persia, Tibet, or some other place, learning magic and mystical secrets. However, the Gospels clearly state that he remained in Nazareth. The people of Nazareth will

later recognize him as the carpenter, not as a world traveler.

The great mystery is that Jesus spent thirty years obeying two humans, three years teaching his disciples, and three hours redeeming the world. Perhaps we can look at the ordinariness of our lives in light of the way Christ saved the world and appreciate the everyday elements more fully.

The Synagogue in Nazareth

To reach the site of the synagogue, it's necessary for pilgrims to walk through a narrow marketplace until they reach the Greek Catholic church. During early trips we usually skipped this site, but now I never miss it. The church is very beautiful, and its Byzantine icons are worth seeing. It stands as a witness to the ancient Byzantine Catholic tradition that still boasts a lively community in Nazareth.

Just past the church is the synagogue. While the building is certainly not from the first century, it may well be built on the site of the ancient synagogue. Here we consider our Lord's rejection by his own people.

Jesus went to Nazareth, where He had been reared, and He entered the synagogue on the Sabbath, as was His custom, and He stood up to read. The book of the Prophet Isaiah was given to Him. Upon opening the book, He found the place where it was written:

"The Spirit of God is upon Me, because He has anointed Me to bring good news to the poor. He has sent Me to announce release to prisoners, and the return of sight to the blind, to send forth the oppressed in freedom, to announce the favorable year of the Lord."

Then rolling up the scroll, He returned it to the attendant and sat down. The eyes of everyone in the synagogue were staring at Him. He began to say to them, "Today this Scripture is fulfilled in your ears."

Everyone testified to Him and wondered at the words of grace that came forth from His mouth. They said, "Is this not the son of Joseph?"

Then He said to them, "Certainly you will quote to Me the saying, 'Physician, heal yourself. The things which we heard have happened in Capernaum, do also here in Your own country.'

"Amen, I say to you that no prophet is accepted in his own country. In truth I say to you, many widows were in Israel in the days of Elijah when the heavens were shut for three years and six months, as there was a great famine upon all the land. But to none of them was Elijah sent, except to Zarephath of Sidon, to a widowed woman.

"Many lepers were in Israel when Elisha was the prophet, but none of them were cleansed except Naaman the Syrian."

Everyone in the synagogue who heard these things was filled with anger. Standing up, they expelled Him from the city and led Him to the brow of the hill on which their city was built, so as to throw Him down. But He walked through their midst and went away.

The marketplace in Nazareth

This was the synagogue where St. Joseph brought the Blessed Virgin Mary and Jesus to pray each Sabbath. This text explicitly mentions that

Jesus knew how to read, and it was probably at the synagogue that he learned this skill along with the other boys of Nazareth. More than knowing

the mechanics of reading, our Lord Jesus obviously reflected on the meaning of Scripture from a very early age, as the time with the elders in the Temple indicates. Just as the teachers in the Temple were "amazed" at his understanding and answers, so now at Nazareth the people of his village are amazed at him.

A danger for Catholics is that we may fall into taking Jesus for granted, much as did the people of Nazareth. If you have been raised in a Christian home, perhaps have attended Christian schools, and, of course, go to church weekly, you may find yourself treating Jesus as if he were just part of the environment. You are familiar with his words and actions, yet neither arouse wonder and amazement. This superficiality prevents vital faith in Jesus.

This same attitude appears when Jesus visits Nazareth at a later stage in his ministry:

Jesus went to His own country, and His disciples followed Him. When it was the Sabbath, He began to teach in the synagogue. Many people listening to Him were amazed.

They said, "From where did these things come to Him? What is the wisdom which has been given to Him? Are such mighty things happening through His hands? Is this not the carpenter, the Son of Mary and the brother of James and Joses, Judah and Simon? Are not His sisters here with us?" They took offense at Him.

Jesus said to them, "A prophet is not dishonored except in his own country, among his own relatives and in his own house."

He was not able to do any miracles there, except lay hands on a few sick people and heal them. He was amazed at their lack of faith.

The people think they know Jesus's parents and relatives, and they take offense at the fact that he is teaching them about the kingdom of God and the eternal salvation of their souls. Their petty theories cause them to miss Christ's message and the power flowing from him.

The names of Jesus's brothers and sisters, among them James and Joses, are mentioned in the Gospels. Both Matthew and Mark mention them in relation to a certain Mary, "the mother of James the younger and of Joses." John tells us that "standing by Jesus's cross were his mother and his mother's sister, Mary the wife of Clopas, and Mary Magdalene." Apparently the "brothers" of Jesus are the children of another Mary, a "sister" of the Blessed Virgin Mary, and her husband, Clopas, rather than children of Joseph and Mary, as some might think.

In the face of this confusion, we seek

Entrance to synagogue at Nazareth

to know the real Jesus of the Gospels. To do so requires that we meditate on him—his words and his actions—with a wonder and amazement that open us to a relationship with him in faith.

Let us pray.
Lord, many of us have grown up with you in our homes, churches, and environment. In some ways we are like the people of Nazareth, and we may even take you for granted. Never let our love for you become the type of familiarity that weakens our faith. Instead, help us always depend on you for everything, seek you first of all, and love you with our whole hearts, minds, and souls.

Cana

Cana is a bustling town with many Christians in it. One particular street has three churches—a Greek Orthodox Church, the Roman Catholic Wedding of Cana Church, and the small Chapel of St. Nathaniel. Along the way are many shops offering icons and souvenirs of the place, including bottles of wine of varying sweetness, dryness, and quality.

The Roman Catholic Church is a wonderful place to consider three aspects of the miraculous event at this location: the miracle of changing the water into wine, the intercession of the Blessed Virgin Mary, and the importance of marriage.

CHAPTER TWENTY-TWO

The Wedding Feast of Cana

On the third day there was a wedding in Cana of Galilee. The mother of Jesus was there, and Jesus and His disciples were invited to the wedding. When the wine ran out, the mother of Jesus said to Him, "They have no wine."

Jesus said to her, "What is it to Me and to you? My hour has not yet come."

His mother said to the servants, "Whatever He says to you, do." Six stone water jars containing eighteen to twenty-seven gallons were in place, for the purification of the Jews.

Jesus said to them, "Fill the jars with water." They filled them to the top. Then He said to them, "Draw some out now and take it to the head waiter." Then they took it.

As the head waiter tasted the water turned wine, though he did not know from where it was (but the servants who drew out the water knew), the head waiter called the groom and said to him, "Every man first offers the good wine, and when they have been drinking, then the lesser. You have kept the good wine until now."

Jesus did the first of the signs in Cana of Galilee, and He manifested His glory. Then his disciples believed in Him.

Right after this event John mentions that the Passover is near. The multiplication of loaves and fish occurs just before the second Passover of the Gospel. We should link these miracles of wine and bread with the institution of the Eucharist at the third Passover of the Gospel.

Notice that Jesus invokes no incantation or fancy actions that would draw attention to the miracle; he simply instructs the servants to take the water to the chief steward and lets the sign take place. Yet his disciples come to believe in him through this hidden and private sign, providing a model for us to follow.

This sign comes at the intercession of Jesus's mother. John's text never names her, though in chapter 19 Jesus invites John and Mary into a close mother-and-son relationship. Neither does John mention his own name but only his relation to Jesus as the "beloved disciple."

Notice also that Mary makes no direct request of Jesus; she simply says the people have no wine. She has obvious trust that he will respond to this embarrassing circumstance; she simply tells the servants to do whatever Jesus tells them.

This, too, provides a model for every believer. Later the Father will give the same message at the Transfiguration: "This is my beloved Son; listen to him." Each of us needs to heed Jesus's mother and Father, listen to Jesus, and obey him.

Wedding Vows

Jesus blesses this marriage with a miracle of abundant good wine, a sign of his blessing of all marriage. This sacrament by which a man and a woman become one flesh is a treasure to each couple who receive it, to their children and families, and to the whole of society. Modern life is becoming more notable for the lack of marriage, which is all the more reason to return to Cana to receive its blessings from Jesus yet again.

A visit to Cana is a good opportunity for married couples to meditate on this sacrament and renew their commitment to one another.

Let us pray.
Will you husbands renew and confirm your taking of your wife in the holy sacrament of matrimony?
I will.
Will you wives renew and confirm your taking of your husband in the holy sacrament of matrimony?
I will.

May the good Lord bless and consecrate the love of husbands and wives. May he bless their rings, which are signs of their continuing love and commitment as they grow in the life of holy matrimony. We ask this through Jesus Christ, the Spouse of his Bride, the Church, and our blessed Lord. Amen.

Let us also pray for the widows and widowers. May God grant eternal life to their spouses who have died. May our Blessed Mother, who attended the wedding feast in this town, intercede for them to make their widowhood holy, filled with wisdom and apostolic ministry and a life of prayer.

Let us pray for those who have experienced divorce. May the Lord who changed the water into wine also transform the pain caused by divorce.

Lord Jesus, you endured the betrayal of Judas and the abandonment by your disciples in Gethsemane. By these hurts, heal any pain still felt by those who have been divorced or by the children from divorced families. May their pain bring healing to others and help strengthen families.

Let us pray for those whom the Lord calls to the single state. May the single members of Christ's Church always remain open to the ways our Lord calls them to his service and ministry. Lord God, we ask that you give them comfort when they feel alone and lead them into deeper union with you and your Church. May the Lord also bless those who are searching for the spouse whom the Lord has in store for them. May they use good discernment in choosing a spouse, and may they seek the mission for their family that the Lord wants them to fulfill. May they maintain a holy chastity until marriage, so that they might remain faithful and true to their spouse and children. Amen.

The topic is his "departure"; the Greek word is *exodus*, a reference to his coming death and Resurrection. Moses and Elijah, who both spoke with God on another mountain, Mount Sinai (called "Horeb" in 1 Kings 19:8–18), now represent the Law and the Prophets, which testify to Jesus as the saving Messiah.

Peter's response is rather confused. He recognizes the goodness of being there, and he wants to make a permanent marker of this event, but he clearly does not know what he is saying. He ends up doing nothing. In fact, when the time of Christ's "departure" arrives, he will even deny knowing Jesus.

Finally, the divine response is an overshadowing cloud and the Father's voice. While the Holy Spirit appeared in the form of a dove at the Jordan River, here he overshadows in a cloud, reminiscent of the overshadowing

cloud in the ancient desert tent containing the ark of the covenant and his overshadowing of the Virgin Mary at Jesus's conception. He surrounds everyone with his pervading presence at this point.

Then, as at the Baptism of Jesus, the Father identifies Jesus as his "beloved Son," a reference to Isaiah 42:1 (a prophet), and then tells the disciples to "listen to him," a reference to Deuteronomy 18:15 (the Law). This simple message from the Father confirms that Jesus fulfills the Law and the

Prophets, as witnessed here on the mountain by Moses and Elijah.

This powerfully dramatic scene ends abruptly and silently. Though the disciples are obviously confused by it all, they will make sense of it later in light of Jesus's death and Resurrection at the end of this journey.

Peter's Account

Another step in making sense of the Transfiguration appears in the second epistle of St. Peter, which retells the episode from the perspective of the late years of Peter's life:

Therefore I intend to remind you always about these things, although you know them and are firm in the present truth. I consider it right, while I am in this tent, to awaken you from sleep, knowing that the removal of my tent is near, as our Lord Jesus Christ revealed to me. I am eager to have you remember these things at any time after my departure.

For we did not follow cleverly devised myths when we made known to you the power and coming of our Lord Jesus Christ, but we were eyewitnesses of His greatness. For He received honor and glory from God the Father, when a voice was addressed to Him by the majestic glory, "This is My beloved Son, in Whom I am well pleased!" And this voice we heard uttered from heaven, having been with Him on the holy mountain.

We have the prophetic word made more firm, to which you do well to pay attention, like a light shining in a dark place until the day dawns and the morning star rises in your hearts.

Know this first: that every prophecy of Scripture is not a matter of private interpretation. For prophecy was not uttered by the will of man then, but rather men spoke, having been brought to speak by the Holy Spirit.

The meaning of St. Peter's life, as it comes to its close, is to pass on for his disciples' remembrance all that he knows about the life of Jesus. He explicitly denies that these stories are "myths," using the Greek term *mythoi*. They are historical events to which he was personally an eyewitness. The specific event he mentions here is the Transfiguration, but he intends all of Christ's life to be known as the truth.

Then Peter states that prophecy is a light shining in our hearts, like the morning star shining before daybreak. While we still look forward to the coming of Christ, we have in Sacred Scripture a bright, fixed point of truth. Scripture is not a matter for private interpretation but the work of the Holy Spirit. We seek there not our personal, human, philosophical insights but God's own truth. The Holy Spirit, whom Jesus identifies as the Spirit of truth, will lead us into all truth and beyond mere human opinion.

Let us pray.
Lord, your Transfiguration was a sign of hope for your disciples as you began to make your way to Jerusalem, the place where you would suffer and die. Moses and the Law, and Elijah and the Prophets, testify to you in this vision, which we cannot see, and in the Scriptures, which we can still read. Open our hearts and minds to receive this testimony about you, especially when we need encouragement. May all the glory be yours forever and ever.

Glory be to the Father, and to the Son, and to the Holy Spirit, as it was in the beginning, is now, and ever shall be, world without end. Amen.

THE SEA OF GALILEE

SEPTENTRIO

MARE
MEDITER
RANEVM

PARS

TRIBVS

Zebulon ad portum marium
ipse ad portu marium habitabit

PARS
TRIBVS

Ptolomais

ROGERO VIVION Mercatori
probe exercitato cujus oculis Syria
notior quam nostro calamo, naves Syria
nautas fetinos, portus fidos, Kolk Ney
tinumq, propitium, omnia denique Zcoulo
nis comoda precatur. T.F.

Beth-lehem

VALLIS

CARMEL

Misheal
ASHER

Canah

VALLIS IEPHTAEL

Hauathon

Hukkok

Bethshemesh

Tepthael

Naasson

Capernaum

Iepthael torrens, sive Shihor Libnah

Iephta torrens

Iordanus Parvus

Aznoth
Tabor

Neah
Remmon
Methoara

Ganereth

PA
TRI
MA

LEVI

Kattah
Kartah

Ajalon

Sepulchrum Elonis

Iokneam

LEVI

Zebulon

Sephoris
(Dionesarea)

Ittah-kazin

Dothaim

Magdala

Gath Hepher

Dalman Atha

ORIENS

SALTVS

CARMELI

Nazareth

Iotopata
Naphteh

MARE
Genezareth
Galilaeæ
Tiberiadis

OCCIDENS

M
MEL

ON
S

Naim

Bethulia

GALILÆÆ
INFERIOR

Caiphas
Kishon flu

CAR
MEL

Cain

Shimron-meron

Kishon flu.

Tiberias

I-nel-Tiger

G

LEVI

Idalah

LEVI

Nahalal
Tabor

Hacthur Dana sicum

A
IN

Rimmon
Dimnah

TABOR MONS

Tarichea

LEVI
sive Kedumim

Dabbasheth

Maralah

Sarid

Kishon flu.

Kishon minor

Chisloth
Tabor

HER MON MONS

Daberah

SCALA   MILLIARIVM

PARS

TRIBVS

MERIDIES

ISHACHAR

1 2 3 4 5 6 7 8 9 10

On the Sea of Galilee

The Sea of Galilee is known by a variety of names. The book of Numbers calls it the Sea of Kinnereth, a word related to the Hebrew word for a harp (*kinnor*). Luke calls it Genesareth, and John refers to it as the Sea of Tiberias, named by Herod Antipas after the Roman Emperor Tiberius. Most of the New Testament calls it the Sea of Galilee, the name that is most familiar to Christians. Since Hebrew does not have many words for various bodies of water, this lake is called a sea.

The lake is freshwater, fed by the Jordan River from the north plus a number of springs, many of which are heated underground. The lake is twelve and a half miles long and seven and a half miles wide. It lies

683 feet below sea level and is 126 feet at its deepest point. At the time of Christ, nine cities and many villages surrounded the lake, including Capernaum, Bethsaida, Magdala, and Tiberias.

To the west of the lake is Mount Arbel, from which a large chunk has fallen off to form the "Valley of the Doves." When the dominant northwesterly winds blow strongly through this narrow gap, they act as a bellows on the lake and cause the sudden storms for which the lake is still famous.

The Sea of Galilee is vibrant with life. At the south end of the lake, the Jordan River continues to flow down (*Jordan* comes from the Hebrew word meaning "to go down") to the Dead Sea, thirteen hundred feet below sea level. Nothing at all can live in its waters, which are 27 percent salt— nine times as salty as the ocean. The Dead Sea receives freshwater from the Jordan but cannot give back, since it is the lowest point on the surface of the earth. The salt has built up, and the sea is dead.

We can draw an important lesson from this fact: The person who receives without giving back becomes spiritually dead, whereas the person who receives God's grace and then gives it away remains spiritually alive and fruitful.

While sailing on the Sea of Galilee, it is good to consider the following three episodes:

Jesus Calls the First Fishers of Men

One time the crowd was pressing upon Jesus in order to hear the word of God. He was standing on the shore of Genesareth, and He saw two boats standing at the shore. The fishermen had disembarked from them and were washing the nets. Getting on board one of the boats, which belonged to Simon, He asked him to put out a little from land. Then Jesus sat in the boat and taught the crowds.

As He rested from speaking, Jesus said to Simon, "Put out into the deeps and lower your nets for a catch."

Simon answered, "Master, after toiling the whole night, we have taken in nothing. But at Your word I will lower the nets."

As they did this, they caught a great number of fish, and their nets were ripping. They signaled to their partners in the other boat to come help them. So they came, and they filled both boats so as to sink them!

Simon Peter fell at Jesus's knees, saying, "Leave me, for I am a sinful man, Lord." For amazement had fallen upon him and all those with him over the catch of fish that they had hauled in. Likewise with James and John, the sons of Zebedee, who were partners with Simon.

Jesus said to Simon, "Fear not. From now on you will be catching men."

After bringing their boats onto land, they left everything and followed Him.

A cove on the lakeshore just south of Capernaum is still known as the Cove of the Parables. It forms a natural amphitheater where a crowd could listen to Jesus speak. The reason for his request to teach from a boat sitting a little off shore is that water amplifies sound, so people could hear him better. The fishermen could continue to mend their nets as they listened to him speak.

Perhaps as a sign of his gratitude for using the boat, Jesus asks Simon to put out into the depths of the lake for a catch. Drawing on his years of experience, and perhaps a bit exasperated by the carpenter-rabbi's suggestion, Peter explains that they have fished all night with no success. (The reason they fish at night is that the fish cannot see the cotton nets falling on them in the dark water.) Yet Peter is willing to follow Jesus's seemingly uninformed word.

To Peter's surprise, he fills his and his partners' boats so full that they are in danger of sinking. In the face of this miraculous catch, Simon is filled with amazement and with remorse for his sinfulness. His experience is common to many saints: The closer they get to God, the more aware they become of their sinfulness.

This is rather like many of us, myself included, who cannot distinguish navy blue, black, or dark brown socks inside our room. Only when we get into the sunlight do we see the color distinctions clearly. So also, when we sinners are among ourselves, we do not notice our faults; but in the sunlight of God's presence, we notice them far more clearly. This is Simon Peter's experience.

As is true throughout the Bible when sinful people meet God, Jesus's response is to assure the men, "Fear not." Jesus then changes Simon's vocation from that of a fisherman to that of a fisher of men. Simon Peter takes on this role, and despite the ups and downs of his relationship with Jesus in the Gospels, he will travel the deeps of the world to accomplish it.

Let us pray.
Lord, you have given us everything we have: our life, our body, our talents, and our strengths. We return it all to you and ask for the privilege of always following you, despite our sinful weakness. Let us accept the deeper vocation you offer us, so that we might become your instruments in spreading your good news to our fellow sinners. Amen.

Jesus Calms the Storm

After He had taught the crowd in parables, and it had become evening, He said to His disciples, "Let us cross to the other side." Leaving the crowd, they took Him along, as He was in the boat, and other boats were with Him.

Then there was a great storm of wind, and the waves beat against the boat, since the boat was already filling up. But He was in the stern, sleeping on a pillow. They woke Him and said to Him, "Teacher, does it not worry You that we are perishing?"

He woke up, rebuked the wind, and said to the sea, "Be quiet; be still." The wind stopped, and there was a great calm. Then He said to them, "Why were you afraid? Do you not yet have faith?"

They were very afraid, and they said to one another, "Then who is this that even the wind and the sea obey Him?"

St. Thérèse of Lisieux, the Little Flower, has a wonderful reflection on this passage. As she was enduring some great difficulties in her life, one of her sisters said, "Why don't you cry out to God for help?"

She responded that, during those difficulties, it did seem as if Jesus were sleeping and ignoring her plight. However, she did not want to wake him in fear, as the disciples did in the boat, lest he rebuke her for having as little faith as they did. He could go on sleeping if he wanted.

Let us pray.
Lord, grant us a trusting faith in you, even when the storms of life are very difficult and it seems as if you are asleep. Help us to trust that you are present in the boat and help us to overcome our fears by faith in your presence. Amen.

The Calling of St. Peter, *by Barna da Siena*

Walking on the Sea of Galilee

After having fed the five thousand, Jesus immediately required the disciples to get into the boat and precede Him to the other side, until He dismissed the crowd. Having dismissed the crowd, He went up the mountain by Himself to pray. When it became evening He was there alone. But the boat was already a few miles distant from land, where it was being battered by the waves, for the wind was against it. In the fourth watch of the night He came to them, walking on the sea.

When the disciples saw Him, they were terrified, saying, "It is a ghost!" They cried out in their fear.

Immediately Jesus said to them, "Take courage; it is I. Do not fear."

Peter answered Him, "Lord, if it is You, command me to come to You upon the water."

Jesus said, "Come."

Upon getting out of the boat, Peter walked on the water and came to Jesus. But when he saw the strong wind, he became afraid. As he began to sink, he cried out, "Lord, save me!"

Immediately Jesus stretched out His hand, lifted him up, and said, "O man of little faith, why did you doubt?" As they got into the boat, the wind stopped.

Those in the boat worshiped Him, saying, "Truly, You are the Son of God!"

This episode points to Christ's divinity in a very special way. In the Old Testament the only one who walked on water was the Lord God. He led the people of Israel through the Red Sea. The Psalms say this: "In the sea was your way, and your path was in the great waters; but your footprints were not known." Job says that God "trampled the waves of the sea." And Isaiah says that the Lord made "the depths of the sea a way for the redeemed to pass over." If Jesus is walking on the water, and then makes it possible for Peter to walk on it with him, then this episode indicates that Jesus is the Lord God.

A second issue is the focus on faith. As long as Peter keeps his eyes on Jesus, he can do the impossible and walk on water. Once he looks at the waves, he sinks.

So often we keep our focus on the problems that assail us, and we, like Peter, sink in them. Here we see the necessity of keeping our attention on Jesus, focusing our lives on him rather than on our problems. Then we can make it through life's many difficulties.

Let us pray.
Lord Jesus, help me develop a habit of keeping my attention on you throughout life—both in the good times, that I might thank you, and in the tough and dangerous times, that I might trust you. Even when I sink into my problems as Peter did, please reach out your hand to me again, and lift me up to walk over the storms of life with you. May I neither be overwhelmed by hardships nor be complacent in good times, but in all times may I be centered on you. Amen.

Capernaum

A stone gate welcomes us to the town of Capernaum, a site owned and excavated by the Franciscans.

The property includes houses made of basalt stone, the ancient synagogue, and the house of Peter's mother-in-law—scenes of a number of important Gospel episodes. The synagogue in Capernaum has two levels to it. Most visible is the beautiful limestone work on the first level. The Jewish community made this improvement around the end of the fourth century A.D.

When standing next to the building, we can see the dark gray basalt belonging to the synagogue of the first century. This is the site of a number of Christ's teachings and deeds.

CHAPTER TWENTY-FIVE

Preaching in Capernaum and an Exorcism

Jesus and his first disciples entered Capernaum. Immediately, on the Sabbath, He went into the synagogue and taught. They were amazed at His teaching, for He taught them as One having authority, and not like the scribes.

A man with an unclean spirit was in their synagogue, who cried out, "What is it to us and to you, Jesus of Nazareth? Have you come to destroy us? We know who you are—the Holy One of God!"

Jesus rebuked him, saying, "Be silent; come out of him." Then the unclean spirit convulsed him and, crying out in a loud voice, came out of him.

Everyone was astonished as they asked each other, "Who is this? What is this new teaching, for it has authority! And he gives orders to unclean spirits and they obey him!" The report about him went out immediately into the whole district of Galilee.

This is the first episode of public ministry that St. Mark reports after the call of the four brothers, Peter and Andrew, James and John. Notice that the reason for the people's amazement is the authority with which Jesus teaches in the town synagogue. One can read in the Mishna and Talmud, which are collections of the sayings of the Pharisaic rabbis, that Rabbi A would cite the opinion of Rabbi B and then cite Rabbi C, whom Rabbi B was quoting. The emphasis in this Pharisaic literature is that the rabbis depended on a line of tradition from earlier rabbis and did not assert their own opinions. Jesus amazes the congregation by teaching on his own authority, without citing other rabbis.

We might pause here and consider the ways we allow the authority of Jesus to have an impact on our lives. Do we treat his word as more authoritative than our own word?

The second part of this episode concerns the demon-possessed man. The evil spirit has more insight into Jesus than do the people in the congregation. It knows of Jesus's mission to destroy the demons and of his identity as the Holy One of God. However, Jesus does not want the demonic forces to give information about his identity, so he rebukes the spirit into silence and commands it to leave the man.

Throughout the Gospels Jesus silences everyone who identifies him, except for the centurion at the cross. This may indicate that, while exorcisms and healings give evidence of Jesus's authority, it will nonetheless be at the cross that the believer can truly understand his divinity. That is the ultimate source of the redemption and the wisdom we receive from him.

The Healing of the Centurion's Servant

After He had finished all of His words in the hearing of the crowd, He entered Capernaum. The servant of a centurion, who was dear to him, was ill, about to come to the end. Having heard about Jesus, the centurion sent some of the elders of the Jews to Him, asking Him to come and heal his servant.

When they reached Jesus, they asked Him earnestly, "He is worthy of having You do this for him, for he loves our people, and he built the synagogue for us."

Jesus went along with them. He was already not far from the house when the centurion sent friends, saying,

"Lord, do not trouble yourself, for I am not worthy that you should come under my roof. Therefore I was not worthy to come to You myself. Only say the word, and my servant will be healed. For I am a man commanded by authority, having soldiers under me. I say to one, 'Go,' and he goes; and to another, 'Come,' and he comes; and to my servant, 'Do this,' and he does it."

Jesus was amazed at this. He turned to the crowd following Him and said, "I say to you, I have not found such faith in Israel!"

Those who had been sent returned to the house and found the servant healed.

The synagogue is a good place to remember this passage, because it is built over the foundation that the centurion constructed out of love for the Jews of Capernaum. Such affection between Romans and Jews was not common. Experiencing it with this centurion motivates the elders to ask Jesus to help the man. The centurion displays humility in the face of Jesus's willingness to help. While the elders consider him worthy of receiving Jesus's help, he does not consider himself worthy of Jesus's visit. But he understands the chain of command that every soldier knows, and he trusts that Jesus's word has the type of power that any commander can exercise.

Jesus responds with amazement at the centurion's faith. His humble faith brings a healing for his servant. We still cite the centurion's words immediately before we receive Holy Communion. We recognize that we are not worthy to have the Lord enter under the roofs of our bodies in this most holy Sacrament, yet we trust in the power of his word to heal us of sin and transform us into worthiness. May the Lord Jesus Christ recognize an act of faith in our humble words, too.

Jesus Teaches About the Bread of Life

When the crowd saw that Jesus was not there, nor were His disciples with Him, they embarked in their boats and went to Capernaum, seeking Jesus. When they found Him across the sea, they said, "Rabbi, when did You come here?"

Jesus answered them and said, "Amen, amen, I say to you, you are seeking Me not because you see signs but because you have eaten from the bread and eaten your fill. Work not for the food that perishes but for the food that remains for eternal life, which the Son of Man will give to you."…

"What must we do to perform the works of God?"

Jesus answered and said to them, "This is the work of God, that you believe in the One Whom He has sent."

"Therefore, what sign do You do so that we may know and believe in You? What do You do? Our fathers ate manna in the desert, as it is written, 'He gave them bread from heaven to eat.'"

"Amen, amen, I say to you, Moses did not give you bread from heaven, but My Father gives you the true bread from heaven. For the bread of God is that which descends from heaven and gives life to the world."

"Lord, always give us this bread!"

"I am the bread of life. Whoever comes to Me will not hunger, and whoever believes in Me will not thirst always. But I said to you that you have seen Me and you did not believe. Everything the Father gives Me comes to Me; and the one who comes to Me I do not drive out. For I have come down from heaven, not that I may do My own will but the will of the One who sends Me. This is the will of the Father who sends Me: that all that He gives to Me I may not lose from Him, but I may raise it up on the last day. This is the will of the One who sends Me, that everyone who sees the Son and believes in Him may have eternal life, and I will raise him up on the last day."

The Judaeans grumbled against Him because He said, "I am the bread that has come down from heaven." And they said, "Is this not Jesus, the son of Joseph, whose father and mother we know? How does He say, 'I have come down from heaven'?"

"Do not murmur among yourselves. No one is able to come to Me unless the Father who sent Me draws him. And I will raise him up on the last day. It is written in the Prophets, 'And all shall be taught by God' [Isaiah 54:13]. Therefore, whoever listens to the Father and learns comes to Me. Not that anyone has seen the Father; only the One who is from God has seen the Father. Amen, amen, I say to you, the one who believes in Me will have eternal life. I am the bread of life. Your fathers ate the manna in the desert, and they died. This is the bread that comes down from heaven, so that

In Jesus's typical style, he meets people at their level and brings them to his deeper teaching. Though they say they are looking for Jesus, he knows that they want more bread. They want to do the works of God, but he calls them to faith in himself. They want a sign, and he offers them the bread of life, his own Body and Blood. They think on the level of cannibalism, and he offers them an understanding of his flesh and blood that is spiritual and will bring them to eternal life in him.

whoever eats of it may not die. I am the living bread Who has come down from heaven. If anyone eats this bread, he will live forever. And the bread that I will give is My flesh, which I will give for the life of the world."

Therefore the Judaeans quarreled among themselves, saying, "How can He give us flesh to eat?"

"Amen, amen, I say to you: Unless you eat the flesh of the Son of Man and drink His blood, you do not have life within you. The one who eats My flesh and drinks My blood has eternal life, and I will raise him up on the last day. For My flesh is truly food, and My blood is truly drink. The one who eats My flesh and drinks My blood remains in Me, and I in him."

St. Peter's House

The site of St. Peter's house is east of the synagogue, past a couple ancient houses and closer to the Sea of Galilee. A modern church, shaped like a fishing boat, is suspended on pillars over an ancient Byzantine church's octagonal walls. Below those walls are parts of a second-century house church and a first-century home. Various graffiti confirm the fact that this home was the residence of St. Peter and therefore of our Lord during his stays in Capernaum. Many important events occurred here or nearby.

Healings and Exorcisms

Immediately after Jesus left the synagogue, He went to the house of Simon and Andrew, along with James and John. Simon's mother-in-law was lying in bed with a fever, so they spoke to Him about her. He went to her and,

grasping her hand, raised her up. The fever left her, and she served them.

When it became evening and the sun set, they brought to Him everyone who had a disease or was demon-possessed. The whole town had gathered in front of the door, and He healed many who had various diseases. He cast out many demons, and He would not let the demons speak, since they knew Him.

The healing of Peter's mother-in-law occurs immediately after the synagogue service in which Jesus cast out the demon. It is the first of a number of Sabbath healings, though since it is private, it causes no controversy.

We can observe that the woman's response to Jesus's healing is to serve others. This is a model for all who are healed and forgiven by Jesus. His saving action toward each of us is meant to evoke a response of loving service to the people around us.

The Paralytic Let Through the Roof

Jesus came again to Capernaum after a few days. People heard that he was at home, and many assembled, so there was no longer any room near the door. He spoke the word to them. They came to Him, bringing a paralytic carried by four people. But not being able to bring him through the crowd, they removed the roof where He was. After they dug through, they lowered the cot on which the paralytic lay.

Jesus, seeing their faith, said to the paralytic, "Child, your sins are forgiven."

Some of the scribes were there and argued in their hearts, "Who is He who speaks in such a way? He blasphemes! Who is able to forgive sins except God?"

Jesus immediately knew in His spirit that they were arguing that way within themselves, so He said, "Why do you dispute these things in your hearts? Which is easier: to say to the paralytic, 'Your sins are forgiven,' or to say, 'Pick

The Paralytic of Capharnaum is Lowered from the Roof, *by the Byzantine School*

up and carry your mat and walk'? So that you may know that the Son of Man has authority to forgive sins on earth," He said to the paralytic, "I say to you, get up, take your mat, and go to your own house."

He got up and immediately picked up his mat and left in front of everyone. Everyone was amazed and glorified God, saying, "We have never seen anything like this!"

Ruins of St. Peter's House

The house at Capernaum is also a scene for teaching. The quick assembly of a crowd indicates how important Jesus's words are. Still, a paralytic seeks physical healing. With the help of his friends, he comes through the roof, which would have been easily replaceable thatch and mud.

Reading and meditating on this passage inside the modern church yields a great perspective on this event. The church is above the ancient house, and the architect designed a glass floor. Thus we can look into the house from the perspective of the paralytic and his friends.

Jesus looks on the event as an act of faith, not only for the friends but also for the paralytic. Yet his pronouncement of forgiveness of sins is doubly surprising. Generally the sick came to Jesus and were simply healed; here a word of forgiveness is offered. The scribes accuse Jesus of blasphemy because only God can forgive. Sin offends God primarily, and thus he needs to effect the reconciliation.

Note that this is not a spoken dispute, but Jesus knows what is in the scribes' hearts. As Psalm 44 says, God "knows the secrets of the heart." Jesus heals the man of the paralysis, to prove that the Son of Man has authority to forgive sins.

The knowledge of human hearts, the power to heal, and the power to forgive sins belong to Jesus precisely because he is God.

The Via Maris

Just east of the church above Peter's house is a roadway that follows the ancient Via Maris, the road that proceeded along the Mediterranean coastline, through a pass leading to the Jezreel Valley, along the Sea of Galilee, and on to Damascus. This is one of the great ancient trade routes that connect Africa, Asia, and Europe. Capernaum was the last town in Herod's territory. Before travelers crossed into the tetrarchy of Philip, a tax collector would take a last-chance toll. The centurion and Roman soldiers in town were insurance for calm, peaceful tax collection.

This is the likely site of Jesus's summons of the first of two tax collectors in the Gospel.

The Call of Levi (Matthew)

Jesus left again, going along the sea, and the whole crowd came to Him, and He taught them. As He went along, He saw Levi, the son of Alphaeus, seated at the tax collector's booth, so He said, "Follow Me."

So he got up and followed Him. As Jesus sat in Levi's house, many tax collectors and sinners were assembled with Jesus and His disciples, for many were there and they followed Him.

When the scribes of the Pharisees saw that He ate with tax collectors and sinners, they said to His disciples, "He is eating with tax collectors and sinners."

Having heard this, Jesus said to them, "The strong do not have need of a doctor, but those who have a disease. I have not come to call the righteous but sinners."

Tax collectors were so despised that families were warned against permitting their children to marry into a family that included one. Nonetheless, Jesus invites one to follow him, just as he has invited the fishermen. Levi accepts as readily as the fishermen did, leaving his post and his past behind.

Levi invites Jesus to his home, and that causes great scandal, as his fellow tax collectors and other sinners join in the table fellowship. This is, in fact, a double scandal. First, table fellowship with a great rabbi was considered a privilege only for chosen disciples. The Talmud contains discussion about who should be permitted to sit in proximity to the rabbi because it was so important an issue. Here Jesus permits sinners to eat with him.

Second, some of the Pharisees believed that the Messiah would come only when every Israelite obeyed every

commandment of God, even for a short duration of time. Therefore the sinners were preventing the Messiah from coming. However, Jesus teaches a radically different doctrine: The Messiah comes for the sinners. Their presence draws him down from heaven, and it is precisely to heal them of sin that he comes. Jesus does not wait until we fix ourselves before calling us; he is the Physician of souls.

Tax in a Fish

When they came to Capernaum, those taking up the half-shekel tax approached Peter and said, "Does your Teacher pay the half-shekel tax?"

He said, "Yes."

When they entered the house, Jesus spoke first. "What do you think, Simon? Do the kings of the earth receive taxes or toll from anyone? Is it from their sons or from strangers?"

Peter said, "From strangers."

Jesus said, "Therefore the sons are free. But so that we do not scandalize them, go to the sea, throw in a fishhook, and when you bring it up, take the first fish. Then open its mouth, and you will find a shekel. Take that and give it to them for you and for Me."

Two conversations occur and would seem unrelated, except for the special kind of knowledge that Jesus regularly exhibits. The first is between Peter and some unnamed Temple officials, who ask whether Jesus pays the Temple tax. At stake is whether Jesus fulfills the whole Law of Moses. Peter answers affirmatively.

But Jesus has something to add. Without having heard the conversation directly, Jesus asks a rhetorical question about whether kings tax their own sons or strangers. Peter gives the obvious answer, it is strangers who pay the tax, and Jesus concludes that sons are free. This comparison is one more implication that Jesus is the Son of God. He is exempt from paying a tax to his Father.

Yet Jesus does not want to cause scandal. Therefore he tells Peter to fish for the money! Again Jesus demonstrates his special knowledge. Further, he trusts that his Father will provide the shekel to pay the tax to the Father's house, the Temple.

Capernaum was a good place for fishing, since a semitropical bass, known today as St. Peter's fish, is common there. The fish lays golden-colored, translucent eggs. The male swims above the eggs to protect them from predators. When a threat appears, the fish scoops up the eggs in its mouth until the danger has passed.

Such a fish might pick up a shiny shekel along with the eggs. Thus, finding a coin inside such a fish is feasible, though not likely by nature. Christ's divine power knows of the shekel in the fish, and his filial relationship with his Father motivates this providence.

Lessons from Capernaum

The many events that took place in this town demonstrate a series of important themes. First, we see the signs of power and the amazing knowledge that point to the divinity of Jesus Christ. Second, we see that people are amazed at his words and deeds because they exceed human expectations. Third, we see the repeated summons to faith in Jesus; we also see some people decide to turn away from him. Fourth, we see his forgiveness of sins and the reconciliation of the repentant to God.

Let us pray.

Lord, grant us the time to reflect on the events of life that evoke amazement at what you are doing with us: the times you save our lives from dangers, prevent us from falling into serious sin, heal us of sickness, and forgive our sins. As we see these events in the light of all you did at Capernaum, grant us a deepening of faith in you that leads to a stronger commitment to you in everyday life.

Help us see the places where we live as our own Capernaum, where we will encounter the sick, disturbed, sinful, and disoriented. May we bring them the same good news that you left with the people of Galilee. Let this word, like the two-edged sword it is, pierce their hearts and bring them to the joy of salvation in you. May this be for your greater glory forever. Amen.

The Mount of Beatitudes

On a hill overlooking the Sea of Galilee, Capernaum, and Tabgha stands the Church of the Beatitudes, built in 1937. This was a deserted district in the first century, fitting the Gospel's description for the location of the Sermon on the Mount. The south side of the Mount of Beatitudes is a natural amphitheater with very good acoustics, a perfect place to address a large crowd.

The Franciscan Sisters take care of the church and its beautiful gardens. There are a number of outdoor altars available for Mass and private meditation.

The Beatitudes

Seeing the crowds, Jesus went up the mountain. When He sat down, His disciples approached Him. Then He opened His mouth and taught them, saying:

"Blessed are the poor in spirit, for theirs is the kingdom of heaven!

"Blessed are the meek, for they shall inherit the earth!

"Blessed are they who hunger and thirst for righteousness, for they shall be satisfied!

"Blessed are the merciful, for they will be shown mercy!

"Blessed are the clean of heart, for they shall see God!

"Blessed are the peacemakers, for they shall be called sons of God!

"Blessed are they who are persecuted for the sake of righteousness, for theirs is the kingdom of heaven!

"Blessed are you when they revile and persecute you and, lying, speak every evil word against you, on account of Me: Rejoice and be glad, for your reward is great in heaven!"

St. Matthew begins with a description of Jesus seated on the hill to teach his disciples and the crowds. The parallel with Moses on Mount Sinai is obvious, and at the same time we see major differences. Moses legislates, and most of the laws are prohibitions of bad behavior: "Thou shalt not...." Jesus instructs on the deeper purpose of life, especially through the Beatitudes. Rather than command specific behaviors, they commend attitudes that will guide a person through life in this world to the final judgment at the end of the world.

Certainly these virtues go contrary to worldly expectations, including those of the modern world:

- The world broadcasts from many quarters the advantages of material wealth. The media in particular hails the houses of the rich and famous, their "bling," their fabulous outfits at major social events. Advertising promotes the acquisition of more goods because we "need" them, "deserve" them, and want to look good. Jesus, on the other hand, promotes poverty of spirit, a type of detachment from the possessions of this world that frees us to use things only insofar as they help us promote the glory of God. The beatitude includes a promise: The "poor in spirit … will inherit the earth."
- The world typically promotes the acquisition of power so that we can influence others. More than one book promotes winning through the intimidation of others. Jesus promotes a meekness that will inherit the earth.
- The world promotes having as much fun as possible and avoiding pain and suffering at almost any cost. Jesus proclaims mourners blessed because of the eternal comfort they will receive.
- The world frequently promotes revenge, while Jesus promises mercy to those who show mercy to others.
- The world makes a huge business of the promotion of many forms of lust, while Jesus promises that the pure of heart will see God. His image is hidden from the lustful.

Jesus doesn't expect his disciples to fit in with the world. Rather we are to be salt to a tasteless world and light to its darkness.

Salt and Light

You are the salt of the earth. But if the salt loses its flavor, with what will it be salted? It is good for nothing except to be thrown outside and be trampled by men!

You are the light of the world. No one is able to hide a city set on a mountain. Nor does anyone light a lamp and put it under a bushel, but on the lampstand, and it lights everything in the house. So let your light shine before men, so that they may see your good works and glorify your Father in heaven.

Jesus goes on to cite various commandments and give them deeper meaning, using a series of contrasts. For example, "You have heard it said, 'Thou shalt not kill,' but I say, whoever is angry with his brother is liable to judgment"; "You have heard it said, 'Thou shalt not commit adultery,' but I say, do not even look at a woman with lust."

Such authority to interpret the Law was not the way of the rabbis, as witnessed in the collection of their sayings in the Mishna and Talmud. Jesus uses his authority to go to the depths of the Law, so that obedience summons a change in the heart. Jesus further assures us that he will reverse everything the world offers in favor of his eternal blessedness. He summons us to see things from his perspective. His words direct our attention to the ultimate purpose of everything, which is God's glory.

Let us pray.

Lord, the world offers me so many promises, even though a steady, wise gaze at these hopes and their fruits shows them to be hollow and even a way to death and self-destruction. Let me hear you in the quiet of this mountaintop. Call me to a greater and eternal glory that the world cannot give and cannot take away.

As you transform me by your promises of eternal life, make me salt that preserves the world from destruction and light that drives away its darkness. May I help bring others to the truth of your blessedness in this life and into eternal life. Amen.

Tabgha: The Church of the Multiplication of the Loaves and Fishes

The Benedictine Church of the Multiplication of the Loaves and Fishes is built over the ruins of two previous churches. The first was built around A.D. 350 by St. Josipus, a Jewish nobleman who converted to Christianity. A Byzantine church was built over the same place around A.D. 480. After its destruction by the Persians in 614, the site was abandoned. German Benedictines excavated the ruins in 1932; they rebuilt the church from 1980 to 1982.

CHAPTER TWENTY-SEVEN

Beneath the altar is a stone on which, according to Jewish Christian tradition, Jesus placed the loaves and fishes. In front of the altar is a mosaic of the loaves and fishes, one of the most famous mosaics in the Holy Land. Along the floor are wonderful ancient mosaics of the birds, animals, and plants of the Sea of Galilee region. Thus, being inside the church is like being outside. This is a good place to meditate on the multiplication of the loaves and fishes.

The Loaves and Fishes

Jesus went to the other side of the Sea of Galilee, which is the Sea of Tiberias. A large crowd followed Him, because they saw the signs that He had done for the sick. Then Jesus went up a mountain, and He sat there with His disciples. This was near the Passover, the feast of the Jews.

Jesus, having raised His eyes and seen that a large crowd was coming toward Him, said to Philip, "Where will we find bread so that they may eat?" He said this to test him, for He knew what He was about to do.

Philip answered Him, "A hundred days' wages worth of bread would not be enough for them, that each receive a small piece!" One of His disciples, Andrew, the brother of Simon Peter, said to Him, "There is here a small boy who has five barley loaves and two fish, but what are these among so many?"

Jesus said, "Make the people recline." There was much grass in the place, so the men reclined, the number being about five thousand. Then Jesus took the bread, and having given thanks, He gave it to those who were reclining, and likewise with the fish, as much as they wanted. When they were full, He said to His disciples, "Gather the leftover fragments so that nothing may be lost."

Therefore they gathered and filled twelve baskets of fragments from the five barley loaves that were left over by those who had eaten. When the disciples saw that He had done a sign, they said, "This One is truly the Prophet who is coming into the world!"

Knowing that they were about to come and seize Him in order to make Him king, Jesus fled again to the mountain alone by Himself.

Mosaic of the loaves and fishes

The crowd followed Jesus to this remote area to receive healings and teaching. When the people are hungry, Jesus has a plan to feed them, but he tests the apostles' faith first. Philip's response is overly practical; Andrew's idea of sharing five loaves and two fish is impractical.

Jesus instructs the people to recline, the usual posture for eating a meal. He then gives thanks over the bread and fish and feeds the five thousand as much as they want, until all are full.

This feeding before the Passover is a sign that the Messiah has arrived: The Messianic banquet is already being shared among the people. The abundance is remarkable: Even the gathered fragments far exceed the original five loaves and two fish.

We see two responses to the miracle. First, the disciples understand the miracle as a sign and accept the fact that Jesus is the "prophet," the one "who is coming into the world." Their analysis is a reference to Messianic prophecies found in Deuteronomy, Genesis, Zechariah, and Malachi. This is a response of faith that will carry these disciples, especially the apostles, through the Eucharistic discourse at Capernaum on the day following this miracle.

The second response is from the crowd: They want to make Jesus their king. Perhaps they also understand the feeding as a Messianic banquet, but they are looking for a political model. They want a king like the Roman emperor, who gives out free bread and perhaps circuses to go with it. Jesus flees; he prefers to be alone rather than accept this political role of Messiah.

In contrast, the following year Jesus will go up to Jerusalem for the final Passover of his public ministry. He will set his face toward the cross and resurrection, which will make him the kind of Messiah he came to be. A sign on top of his cross will proclaim him publicly as "the King of the Jews."

Let us pray.
Lord, by your word of blessing and thanksgiving, you fed the people who listened to your word. Nourish us by your word proclaimed in Sacred Scripture and by the Bread of Life with which you feed us at the Eucharist. Thus strengthened and made wise, may we dedicate ourselves to your greater praise and glory. Amen.

Church of the Primacy of St. Peter

A green and shaded Franciscan property adjoins the Benedictines' Church of the Multiplication of the Loaves and Fishes and looks over an ancient harbor on the Sea of Galilee. The large rocks placed as a breakwater and the huge boulder with cut steps for an old wharf indicate that the water was once higher than at present. Here the Church of the Primacy of St. Peter commemorates the appearance of Jesus Christ to some of his disciples after the Resurrection.

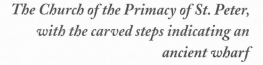

The Church of the Primacy of St. Peter, with the carved steps indicating an ancient wharf

CHAPTER TWENTY-EIGHT

"Peter, do you love me?"

Jesus Appears to His Disciples

Later Jesus manifested Himself again to the disciples at the Sea of Tiberias. He manifested Himself in this way. Simon Peter, Thomas, who was called the Twin, Nathaniel from Cana of Galilee, the sons of Zebedee, and two other of His disciples were together. Simon Peter said to them,

"I am going fishing."

They said to him, "We will go with you."

They went and got into the boat immediately, and in that night they caught nothing. When it was already dawn, Jesus stood on the shore. However, the disciples did not know that it was Jesus. Jesus said to them,

"Lads, don't you have any fish?"

They answered Him, "No."

He said to them, "Cast the net on the right side of the boat, and you will find something."

Then they cast the net, but they were not able to haul it in on account of the large number of fish. The disciple whom Jesus loved said to Peter, "It is the Lord!"

When Simon Peter heard it was the Lord, he wrapped himself in his outer garment—for he was naked—and threw himself into the sea. The other disciples came in the boat—for they were not far from the land, only about one hundred yards—dragging the net. When they disembarked on land, they saw a charcoal fire prepared and fish and bread set out. Jesus said to them, "Bring some of the fish you caught just now."

Simon Peter got up and dragged the net full of one hundred and fifty-three large fish onto land. That being so, the net was not torn. Jesus said to them, "Come, eat breakfast."

None of the disciples dared to ask Him, "Who are You?" They knew that it was the Lord. Jesus came and took the bread and gave it to them, and likewise with the fish. This was already the third time Jesus appeared to His disciples after having been raised from the dead.

"Mensa Christi," meaning "the table of Christ," marks the reock where Jesus shared a meal with his disciples on the shores of the Sea of Galilee following his resurrection

This passage has obvious links with episodes during Jesus's public ministry. The most obvious is with the great catch of fish in Luke, which nearly sank the fishing boats. However, this connection also highlights the great danger Peter's decision to go fishing entailed.

Jesus called Simon Peter and his partners to become fishers of men. Now, after having seen Jesus raised from the dead in Jerusalem, they return to Galilee and go back to fishing for fish. The miraculous catch directed by the Risen Jesus reminds them of the original miracle and their earlier call.

A second link is with the multiplication of loaves and fish in the very same area. Once again they share a meal of bread and fish with Jesus, a sort of Messianic banquet. Only this time Jesus is the Risen Lord present in their midst.

We see two additional links to Jesus's public ministry in his private conversation with Peter.

Peter's Affirmations

When they had eaten breakfast, Jesus said to Simon Peter, "Simon, son of Jonah, do you love Me more than these?"

"Yes, Lord, You know that I love You."

He said to him, "Feed My lambs."

He said to him a second time, "Simon, son of Jonah, do you love Me?"

"Yes, Lord, You know that I love You."

He said to him, "Shepherd My sheep."

He said to him a third time, "Simon, son of Jonah, do you love Me?

Peter was sad because He said to him a third time, "Do you love Me?" and he said to Him, "Lord, You know everything, You know that I love You!"

"Feed My sheep. Amen, amen, I say to you, when you were younger, you girded yourself and went where you wanted. But when you are old, you will stretch out your hands, and another will gird you, and he will take you where you do not want to go."

He said this to indicate by what kind of death he would glorify God. Then He said, "Come, follow Me."

Outdoor chapel

The third link is the obvious connection between Jesus's threefold questioning of Simon's love with his previous denials in the high priest's courtyard. Jesus allows Peter to undo each denial, with a profession not of regret but of love for Jesus.

Fourth, Jesus no longer speaks to Peter about being a fisher of men; rather he is a shepherd of his sheep. Perhaps this change of image for Church leadership will make clearer the complete change Jesus wants to effect in Peter. The image of shepherd goes back to John 10, where Jesus describes himself as the Good Shepherd who lays down his life for his sheep. Now he commands Peter to be a shepherd such as this.

Jesus even indicates that Peter will die a martyr while taking this role of shepherd, much as Jesus did. Tradition says that under Nero, Peter, too, was crucified, only upside down.

Popes Paul VI, John Paul II, and Benedict XVI visited this place during their pilgrimages to the Holy Land, to remind themselves that they continue the same ministry as shepherds of Jesus's sheep. Mosaics commemorate their visits and remind us to pray for the popes in their ministry. Let us pray an Our Father, Hail Mary, and Glory Be for the present pope, that he may be ever faithful in his service to our Lord and his Church.

We also can consider here the fact that each of us receives a call to shepherd other Christians in our care. Our children, students, clients, patients, and others are Christ's sheep, and he wants us to care for them for his sake, not our own.

Let us pray.

Lord, help us to care for the lambs and sheep you have placed in our care. May we seek only their true good and your greater glory in the service we render you through shepherding them. Grant us your wisdom and understanding to know best how to care for others. Give us the courage and fortitude of good shepherds who withstand the wolves and thieves who seek evil for others.

When you seek an account of our leadership and care of others, be merciful to us. Always guide us yourself, and grant us a trust in the legitimate shepherds you have placed over us all. Amen.

The Jordan River

On the Israeli side of the Jordan River there are two sites that commemorate the Baptism of Jesus. Yardenit is near the place where the Jordan flows from the Sea of Galilee. Another site, near Jericho, is the original location of Jesus's Bbaptism. Opposite this, on the Jordanian side of the river, are the ruins of an ancient Byzantine church commemorating the Baptism, along with several modern churches for Catholics, Orthodox, and other Christians.

People went to Yardenit for years because the other site, part of an international border, was closed to pilgrims. Now both sites are open and can be visited for prayer, renewal of baptismal vows, and the baptisms of catechumens.

*Fr. Mitch Pacwa on the shore
of the Jordan River*

221

The Baptism of Jesus

It is written in Isaiah the prophet,

"Behold, I am sending My messenger before your face, who will prepare your way before you. A voice cries in the wilderness, 'Prepare the way of the Lord, make straight His paths.'"

John was baptizing in the wilderness and was preaching a baptism of repentance for the forgiveness of sins. The whole region of Judea and the inhabitants of Jerusalem came out to him, confessing their sins. John was clothed in camel hair and had a leather belt around his waist, and he ate locusts and wild honey. He proclaimed:

"One who is stronger than I is coming after me, of whom I am not worthy to bend down and loosen the strap of his sandal. I baptize you in water; he will baptize you in the Holy Spirit."

It happened in those days that Jesus came from Nazareth of Galilee and was baptized by John in the Jordan.

Immediately after coming up from the water, He saw the heavens opened and the Spirit, like a dove, coming down upon Him. A voice came from heaven, saying,

"This is My beloved Son, in whom I am well pleased."

All four Gospels identify John the Baptist with the voice crying out "in the wilderness" mentioned in Isaiah. Interestingly, this is also the passage most often cited in the Dead Sea Scrolls to identify the desert community of Qumran, located just over five miles from the place of John's baptizing and preaching activity. While the community at Qumran was very exclusive, seeing its own members as the redeemed elite, John appeals to sinners. He cries for repentance and announces the coming of a mighty Messiah.

Mark also cites the third chapter of Malachi to identify John with the messenger who goes before the Lord. This helps distinguish John's role of preparing the way from the coming of the Lord himself. This verse points to Jesus as the Lord God, while John is merely a prophetic messenger preparing for the powerful Lord to come.

Mark's description of John's clothing of camel hair, with a leather belt, further portrays him as Elijah, who used the same tailoring. Malachi was the one who prophesied that Elijah would come before the Messiah, and Jesus indicates that John fulfills that role.

Jesus is baptized, but not for the forgiveness of his sins, as he is like us in all things except sin. The Church Fathers say that when Jesus was baptized, he was not sanctified by the waters, but the waters were sanctified by him, making all water a powerful sign for the baptism of sinners.

At the point of Jesus's Baptism, the heavens open, and the Blessed Trinity is revealed in public: The Holy Spirit hovers in the form of a dove, the Son is baptized, and the Father proclaims the Son to indicate that he is the Messiah who fulfills the prophecies. This manifestation of the Trinity at Jesus's Baptism prepares for the Trinitarian formula for Christian baptism that Jesus will teach later in Matthew: "Go therefore and make disciples of all nations, baptizing them in the name of the Father, the Son, and the Holy Spirit." Both the outward sign of baptizing and the new relationship with the Blessed Trinity are rooted in Jesus Christ's Baptism at the Jordan.

Let us pray.

Father in heaven, you revealed the wonders of baptism with signs at the River Jordan. You made your voice heard from heaven, to stir up faith that Jesus is the Word made flesh. You sent the Holy Spirit in the form of a dove, to reveal Jesus as your beloved Son and to anoint him with joy as the Messiah who was sent to bring the Good News of salvation to the poor. May we always profess our faith in you, the one God—Father, Son, and Holy Spirit—revealed on the banks of the Jordan River. Amen.

Renewal of Baptism

St. Paul teaches us that there is "one Lord, one faith, one baptism, one God and Father of all, who is above all and through all and in all." Let us renew our baptismal promises by rejecting Satan and his works and by professing our faith in God and our willingness to serve him in his holy Catholic Church.

Let us pray.

Do you reject sin, so as to live in the freedom of the children of God?
I do.

Do you reject the glamour of evil and refuse to be mastered by sin?
I do.

Do you reject Satan, father of sin and prince of darkness?
I do.

Do you believe in God, the Father Almighty, Creator of heaven and earth?
I do.

Do you believe in Jesus Christ, his only Son, our Lord, who was born of the Virgin Mary, was crucified, died, and was buried, rose from the dead and is now seated at the right hand of the Father?
I do.

Do you believe in the Holy Spirit, the holy Catholic Church, the communion of saints, the forgiveness of sins, the resurrection of the body, and life everlasting?
I do.

God, the Almighty Father of our Lord Jesus Christ, has given us a new birth by water and the Holy Spirit and forgiven all our sins. May he also keep us faithful to our Lord Jesus Christ for ever and ever.
Amen.

Pilgrims frequently wade into the river or are sprinkled with its water as part of this renewal.

Modern pilgrims can be baptized at this site in the Jordan River

John's Recognition of Jesus, the Lamb of God

We can meditate on the next episode in the life of John the Baptist at Yardenit in the north, to which John seems to have moved after having baptized in Judea. This site is not far from the ancient town of Betanea, which may be the Bethany to which John 1:28 refers. We also read about John baptizing at another location, "Aenon near Salim." His was an itinerant baptizing mission to sinners.

St. John the evangelist tells about John the Baptist's testimony to some priests and Levites sent from Jerusalem to question him after the Lord's baptism.

"Who are you?" they asked.

John confessed, "I am not the Christ."

They asked him, "Who then? Are you Elijah?"

He answered, "I am not."

They asked him then, "Who are you, so that we may give an answer to the ones who sent us. What do you say about yourself?"

He said, "Say, I am a voice crying in the wilderness, 'Prepare the way of the Lord,' as Isaiah the prophet said."

There were also some who were sent by the Pharisees, who asked him: "Why, therefore, do you baptize if you are neither the Christ, nor Elijah, nor one of the prophets?"

John answered them, "I am baptizing in water. One is standing in your midst, whom you do not know. He is the One who has come after me, who existed before me. Of Him I am not worthy to loosen the strap of His sandal."

These things happened in Bethany, across the Jordan, where John was baptizing. The next day John saw Jesus coming toward him and said,

"Behold the Lamb of God, who takes away the sin of the world! This is the One about whom I said, 'After me is coming a man who existed before me, for He was ahead of me.' I did not know Him, but so that He might be manifested to Israel, for this I came baptizing in water. I saw the Spirit coming down as a dove from heaven, and He remained upon Him. I did not know Him, but the One who sent me to baptize said, 'On whomever you see the Spirit coming down and remaining upon Him, that One is the One who baptizes in the Holy Spirit.' And I have seen and have testified that this One is the Son of God."

While John's Gospel does not include a description of Jesus's Baptism, we can assume that it has already taken place. This episode comes just before Jesus calls his first disciples, so we can also assume that the temptations in the wilderness have occurred. The double intention of this passage is to identify who John and Jesus really are.

Two different groups question John. Priests and Levites from the temple ask if he is the Christ, Elijah, or one of the prophets, all of which he denies. As in the other Gospels, he identifies himself as the voice crying in the wilderness. This helps contrast him with Jesus, who is identified as the Word of God, who is God and has become flesh.

Later Jesus will call John a "burning, shining lamp," while Jesus refers to himself as the light of the world. Jesus is the Bridegroom, while John is the groom's friend, who must decrease while the groom increases. John's humble acceptance of Christ's greatness and his own smallness is a model for every Christian: We are to keep Jesus at the center of our life.

The second group to question John here are the Pharisees. They want to understand why John baptizes.

He responds with a focus on the greatness of Jesus, who comes after him yet existed before him. This answer is yet another recognition by John that Jesus is far superior to himself, a fact that echoes the teaching about Jesus in John the evangelist's prologue.

Then John sees Jesus walking by and identifies him as the "Lamb of God who takes away the sins of the world." This can best be understood from the perspective of Jesus's death on the day of the Passover preparation. John quotes, "Not a bone of his shall be broken," in describing the stabbing of Jesus with the soldier's lance, rather than the breaking of his legs, as with the two thieves. This refers to the prohibition against breaking the Passover lamb's bones mentioned in Exodus and Numbers. It is a further claim that Jesus, who dies around the time of the slaying of the Passover lambs in the Temple on the Preparation Day, is the true Lamb of God, just as the Baptist proclaims.

Unlike the lambs slaughtered in the Temple, Jesus takes away the sins of the world. This is a proclamation so important that we include it in our prayers at Mass, right before receiving Jesus in the Eucharist: "Lamb of God, who takes away the sins of the world, have mercy on us…."

Let us pray.
Lord Jesus, you are the Lamb of God who takes away the sins of the world. You died at three o'clock as the Passover was about to begin, just as the priests killed their Passover lambs. May we, the sheep of your pasture, always follow you. May we always turn to you for the forgiveness of our sins, for you are Lord forever and ever. Amen.

Caesarea Philippi

The ruins of Caesarea Philippi are at Banyas, located at the base of Mount Hermon near the Israeli-Lebanese border. The excavations of this city are still incomplete, but visitors always notice the large rock cliff against which the city was built.

From a large cave at the base of the cliff flows one of the three springs—the largest, in fact—that come together to form the Jordan River. The ancient name of this spring was the Gates of Hades. The spring was so deep that no one had ever reached the bottom of it. This information helps us understand some of what Jesus spoke to St. Peter here.

The Gates of Hades

CHAPTER THIRTY

St. Peter's Confession

When Jesus went into the district of Caesarea Philippi, He asked His disciples, "Who do people say the Son of Man is?"

They said, "Some say John the Baptist, others say Elijah, and others say Jeremiah or one of the prophets."

He said to them, "And you, who do you say I am?"

Simon Peter answered, "You are the Christ, the Son of the living God."

Jesus answered by saying, "Blessed are you, Simon son of Jonah, because flesh and blood have not revealed this to you but My Father, who is in heaven. And I say to you, you are Rock, and on this rock I will build My Church, and the gates of hell shall not prevail against it. I will give to you the keys of the kingdom of heaven, and anything you bind on earth will be bound in heaven, and anything you loose on earth shall be loosed in heaven." Then He commanded the disciples not to tell anyone that He was the Christ.

Note that Jesus asks about the "democratic opinion" of his identity, and the popular answers are all wrong. When he asks the apostles who they think he is, the truth is revealed by Simon, son of Jonah, as a gift of the Father. The truth about God is not a human invention but a gift from him.

The truth is that Jesus is both Christ, the Greek translation of "Messiah," and the Son of God. He is the one promised by the prophets, and yet his divinity is more than the prophets could have expected. Surely Peter could not have invented this idea on his own.

Jesus responds with a beatitude directed to Simon, not because the apostle is clever but because the Father has chosen him to reveal the truth about Jesus. This beatitude entails a change of name and identity: Simon is now the Rock (Peter, or *Cephas* in Aramaic), and Jesus will build his Church on this Rock.

The large cliff behind Caesarea is a model for Peter the Rock. The cave of the large spring, the Gates of Hades, is a symbol of the inherent failure of the enemies of the Church to prevail against it.

Another component of Peter's personal beatitude is that Jesus gives him the keys to the kingdom, so that he might have the power to bind and loose. The bestowal of keys was a symbol for making someone the prime minister of the nation. While Jesus is the King, the Messiah and Son of David, Peter is the equivalent of the prime minister. Leading rabbis used the words *bind* and *loose* to commission their disciples with authority over distant communities. Jesus now gives these powers to Peter.

Let us pray.

Lord, grant us the gift of faith, so that we might accept you on your own terms, without any admixture of human opinion. Keep us committed to the truth you are and the truths you reveal.

Keep our Holy Father the pope faithful to your truth, so that he might exercise the authority you give him for the good of his soul and of all souls in the Church and the world. Help us to follow the pope's guidance in your name and solely for your glory.

We trust that the forces of evil and death will never prevail against your Church, not because of our strength but because of your promise. Keep her strong in you, that she might win the wicked over to your goodness. Amen.

The First Prediction of Christ's Death and Resurrection

After that, Jesus began to show his disciples that it was necessary for Him to go to Jerusalem, suffer much from the elders, chief priests, and scribes, and be put to death, and on the third day be raised up.

Peter took Him aside and began to rebuke Him, saying, "May God be good to You, Lord! Do not let this happen to You!"

Turning around, He said to Peter, "Get behind Me, Satan; you are My stumbling block, because you are not thinking the things of God but the things of men." Then Jesus said to His disciples,

"If anyone wishes to come after Me, let him deny himself and take up his cross and follow Me. For if someone wishes to save his soul, he will lose it. But if someone loses his life for My sake, he will find it. For what will it profit a man if he gains the whole world but loses his soul? Or what will a man give in exchange for his soul? For the Son of Man will come in the glory of His Father with His angels, and then He will repay each person according to his deeds."

Immediately after the great beatitude filled with promise for Peter and the Church, Jesus reveals another truth about his Messiahship: He will suffer, die, and be raised from the dead. That revelation does not compute for Peter at all; he is still high on the great promises, including the one that said the forces of death would not prevail against the Church. How could death then defeat the Messiah?

Peter does not yet understand the meaning of Christ's Resurrection. His newly given authority goes to his head, and he rebukes Jesus for speaking the truth about his coming glory. Jesus responds with a sharper rebuke, addressing Peter as "Satan" for contradicting the truth.

This will not be the last failure in Peter's life or in the history of the papacy. Many saints, and history itself, will rebuke Peter's successors for wrongdoing. Still, as Jesus retains Peter's position of leadership throughout the Gospels, the popes remain the Vicars of Christ throughout history.

Jesus turns to all of his disciples, including we who read these words today, and teaches that denying oneself, taking up the cross, and following Jesus are absolute necessities for being a disciple. This way of life contains a promise of eternal life for the soul, when Jesus returns in glory with all his angels to judge everyone according to his or her deeds. This is a promise we must hold dear. May we keep the hope of eternal glory in mind as we offer up the paltry things of this world for the sake of the kingdom of God.

A Final Word

I have been privileged to visit the Holy Land frequently since 1982. I have brought groups to all the sites described in this book, in addition to places for which we had no space. What brings me back to the Holy Land year after year?

First, a familiarity with the texts of Sacred Scripture, both Old and New Testaments, gives me a thirst to know this land. God did not reveal himself in a mythological time and place but in specific times of history and in specific places. Visiting those sites and seeing the ruins of those ancient times changes the places in the Bible into a known, recognizable reality that adds context and a certain familiarity to reading Scripture.

Second, my many trips to the Holy Land have helped me pull together a strong sense of the geography of the land. Not only is it visiting the actual sites, but the travel during which the connection between places is made. Such an understanding did not sink in until my third trip, and repeated visits confirms it. I hope that you can return to this book and its pictures many times in order to gain a more imaginative sense of these holy places. If you have been to the Holy Land yourself, I hope the book helps remind you of the scenery and art so they can continue to teach you as they have taught me.

Third, familiarity with the Holy Land contributes to an understanding and thirst to know the Scriptures. I am always gratified to hear that pilgrims have enjoyed their trip with me, but that pales in comparison to hearing them say, usually with great excitement, "When I hear the Scriptures read at Mass, or when I read them on my own, I can picture what is happening because I was there!"

A Holy Land pilgrimage is meant to draw us into understanding the Bible better so that we can come to know God better. Since most people do not have the chance to visit the Holy Land, I offer this book as a small help to fire your imagination with the reality of the places where God met real human beings and effected their salvation (and ours) within a concrete history. May the Holy Spirit who inspired the sacred authors to write the Old and New Testaments continue his work of filling your hearts and minds with new insights into his revelation in Sacred Scripture. May he bring you to know our Lord Jesus Christ more deeply and through him help you to know our Father in heaven. God bless you.

List of Illustrations

All photos, unless otherwise noted, are from Fr. Mitch Pacwa's private collection. Many thanks to John King and Mac Rojo, who made their photos of the Holy Land pilgrimage available for this book.

Scripture Index

Index